Beginner's
PORTUGUESE

AN EASY INTRODUCTION

DISCARD

Sue Tyson-Ward

TEACH YOURSELF BOOKS

Dedication

For Mum and Dad

Acknowledgements

Many thanks to Mrs Brenda Wright, for her patient typing efforts, and to Mrs Maria Gilham for her valuable comments.

For UK orders queries: please contact Bookpoint Ltd, 39 Milton Park, Abingdon, Oxon OX14 4TD. Telephone: (44) 01235 400414, Fax: (44) 01235 400454. Lines are open from 9.00-6.00, Monday to Saturday, with a 24 hour message answering service. Email address: orders@bookpoint.co.uk

For U.S.A. & Canada order queries: please contact NTC/Contemporary Publishing, 4255 West Touhy Avenue, Lincolnwood, Illionois 60646-1975, U.S.A. Telephone: (847) 679 5500, Fax: (847) 679 2494.

Long-renowned as the authoritative source for self-guided learning – with more than 30 million copies sold worldwide – the *Teach Yourself* series includes over 200 titles in the fields of languages, crafts, hobbies, sports, and other leisure activities.

British Library Cataloguing in Publication Data
A Catalogue record for this title is available from the British Library

Library of Congress Catalog Card Number: 92-68478

First published in UK 1996 by Hodder Headline Plc, 338 Euston Road, London NW1 3BH.

First published in US 1996 by NTC/Contemporary Publishing, 4255 West Touhy Avenue, Lincolnwood (Chicago), Illinois 60646 – 1975 U.S.A.

The 'Teach Yourself' name and logo are registered trade marks of Hodder & Stoughton Ltd in the UK.

Copyright © 1983, 1996 Sue Tyson-Ward

Typeset by Transet Ltd, Coventry.
Printed in Great Britain for Hodder & Stoughton Educational, a division of Hodder Headline Plc, 338 Euston Road, London NW1 3BH by Cox & Wyman Ltd, Reading, Berkshire.

Impression number	10 9 8 7 6 5 4 3				
Year	2002 2001 2000 1999 1998 1997				

CONTENTS

ABOUT THE COURSE

Teach Yourself Beginner's Portuguese is the right course for you if you are a complete beginner or wanting to make a fresh start. It is a self-study course which will help you to understand, read and speak most of the Portuguese you will need on holiday or a business trip.

The book has two parts. The first ten units introduce you to the basic structures and grammatical points you'll need in everyday situations. Units 1–10 should be taken in order as each builds on the previous one.

Units 11–19 deal with everyday situations such as shopping, eating, booking a room, travelling and give you the opportunity to put into practice the language you've acquired in the first part. These units may be taken in any order.

The course is best used together with the accompanying 90-minute audio cassette, but is not dependent upon it. You are recommended to obtain and use the cassette if possible. The recorded dialogues and audio exercises give you plenty of practice in understanding the basic language; they will help you develop an authentic accent and increase your confidence in saying simple phrases. When you are learning a language, particularly in the early stages, there always seem to be long lists of words to wade through. Try to develop your own, efficient, ways of learning vocabulary. Stickers on items around the house, short lists of 'three words a day', memory techniques like mnemonics (visual prompts), making up rhymes, and learning words incorporated into phrases or sentences rather than as individual words out of context. Every person has their own way of learning and you must find the best way for you.

About Units 1–10

Each unit covers approximately ten pages.

The first page tells you what you are going to learn and there is an easy exercise which gets you speaking straight away.

Palavras chaves contain the most important words and phrases from the unit. Try to learn them by heart. They will be practised in the rest of the unit and the later units.

Diálogo. Listen to the dialogues once or twice without stopping the tape or read through it without looking anything up; try to get the gist of it. The notes underneath each dialogue will help you to understand it. Then, using the pause button on your cassette recorder, break the dialogue into manageable chunks and try repeating each phrase aloud. This will help you acquire a more authentic accent.

Leitura and **Monologue**. Listen to these on your cassette, checking you can get the gist of the passage first. Then make sure you know all the vocabulary.

Para estudar. In this section, you may want to start by reading the example(s) then work out the grammatical point or you may prefer to read the **Para estudar** first and see how the rule applies. Once you feel confident about a particular grammar point, try to create your own examples.

Comentário. This section will help you understand the language by explaining differences due to cultural background and changes.

Actividade (*exercise*). Each activity, in this section, allows you to practise one of the points introduced in the **Para estudar** section. In some activities you will need to listen to the cassette. It is not essential to have the cassette in order to complete this course, as most of the activities are not dependent on it. However, listening to the cassette will make your learning much easier.

Avaliação. At the end of each unit you can test yourself on the last two or three unit(s).

About Units 11–19

Each unit covers approximately eight pages.

The first page tells you what you are going to learn. There is also a checklist of structures which you have already learnt and will be practising in the unit. You'll also find in many units a short text in Portuguese about the topic.

Palavras chaves contain the basic vocabulary you'll need when coping, in real life, with practical situations such as checking into a hotel, ordering a snack, asking for a train timetable, going on an excursion.

Diálogos. There are several short dialogues, each dealing with a different aspect of the topic. Remember to listen to the dialogues first and use the pause button to practise the new words and phrases out loud.

Actividades. The activities are mostly based on authentic Portuguese material. Here you can develop a feel for how things work in Portugal, as well as practising your reading skills. You will then have more confidence to cope with the real situations.

Answers

The answers to all the **Actividades**, **Documentos** and **Avaliação** can be found at the back of the book.

Be successful at learning languages

1 **Do a little bit every day**, between 20 and 30 minutes if possible, rather than 2 or 3 hours in one session.
2 **Try to work towards short-term goals**: for example, work out how long you'll spend on a particular unit and work within this time limit.
3 **Revise and test yourself regularly** using the Avaliação at the end of each unit.
4 **Make use of the tips** given in the book and try to say the words and phrases out loud whenever possible.
5 **Try every opportunity to speak the language**. Attend some classes to practise your Portuguese with other people, get some help from a Portuguese speaker or find out about Portuguese clubs, societies, etc.

6 Don't worry too much about making mistakes. The important thing is to get your meaning across and remember that making mistakes in Portuguese will not stop a Portuguese person understanding you. Learning can be fun particularly when you find you can use what you have learnt in real situations.

At the back of the book

At the back of the book is a reference section which contains:

—— Symbols and abbreviations ——

This indicates that the cassette is needed for the following section.

This indicates dialogue.

This indicates exercises – places where you can practise using the language.

This indicates grammar or explanations – the nuts and bolts of the language.

This indicates key words or phrases.

This draws your attention to points to be noted.

This refers you to another page giving further information on a point.

(m)	masculine
(f)	feminine
(sing)	singular
(pl)	plural
(lit)	literally

About the cassette

Although this book can successfully be used on its own, the purchase of the cassette will enhance both your pronunciation and your comprehension abilities as well as giving you the opportunity for aural revision.

Pronunciation guide

 In native Portuguese words there is no **k**, **w**, or **y**, although they appear in imported words. However, there are three double letters which do not exist as such in English.

- The first is **ch**, which is pronounced as in the English *shout*: **chocolate**, **chamar**.
- The second is **lh**, which is pronounced like the *lli* in *billion*: **mulher**, **trabalhar**.
- The third example is **nh**, pronounced like the *ni* in *onion*: **vinho**, **sozinho**.

So the whole Portuguese alphabet is as follows. If you have the cassette, listen to how it sounds when recited in Portuguese.

a b c ch d e f g h i j (k) l lh m n nh o p
q r s t u v (w) x (y) z

Portuguese vowels

Portuguese vowels sounds are tricky to imitate, as Portuguese people 'eat' their words, and particularly, the vowels. There are nasal sounds, and sounds differ depending on where the vowel is in any given word. Here is a general idea:

a, as in *rather* – **falar**	or as in *abide* – **mesa**
ã, as in *rang* – **irmã**.	This is a nasal sound.
e, as in *bell* – **certo**	or as in *madden* – **pesar**
i, as in *mean* – **partida**	or as in *cigar* – **emigrar**
o, as in *saw* – **nova**	or as in *boot* – **sapato**
u, as in *boot* – **durmo**	or as in *bull* – **mudar**

Portuguese consonants also differ from the English sounds in different situations. Follow the table on the cassette, if you have it, as each consonant is given an English equivalent, and a Portuguese example:

Consonant	English sound	Portuguese sound
b	*ball*	bonito
c+a/o/u	*can*	comer
d	*dab*	dar
g + e/i	*pleasure*	geléia
h	'silent'	hotel
l	*last*	livre
m	*map*	mesa
nh	o*ni*on	vinho
q (u)	*quart*	quando
r	'rolled'	rio
s + vowels	*zoo*	casa
ch	*shout*	chocolate
f	*fat*	falar
g + a/o/u	*got*	pagar
j	*pleasure*	julho
lh	bi*lli*on	mulher
n	*nod*	nadar
p	*pin*	parar
q(u) + e/i	'silent u'	quem
s	*sat*	sol
t	*tap*	todo
x	*shout*	baixa
z	*zoo* / *shout*	fazer/faz

The stress rules

Portuguese words are stressed on the last syllable if they end in **i**, **u**, diphthongs, consonants, and nasal vowels: **papel**, **irmão**.

They are stressed on the syllable before last if they are verbs ending in **am** or **em**, or words ending in **a, e, o, em, ens** – **mesa**, **falam**.

If a word breaks either of these rules, a written accent is added to show where the stress falls. So if you see a word with a written accent, you must stress the syllable where the accent is placed.

A few tips to help you acquire an authentic accent

It is not absolutely vital to acquire a perfect accent. The aim is to be understood; here are a number of techniques for working on your pronunciation:

1 Listen carefully to the cassette or native speaker or teacher. Whenever possible repeat aloud imagining you are a native speaker of Portuguese.

2 Tape record yourself and compare your pronunciation with that of a native speaker.

3 Ask native speakers to listen to your pronunciation and tell you how to improve it.

4 Ask native speakers how a specific sound is formed. Watch them and practise at home in front of a mirror.

5 Make a list of words that give you pronunciation trouble and practise them.

Now practise your pronunciation by saying these place names (if you have the cassette listen to each one first), and look them up on the map, to see where each place is in Portugal.

First of all, the regions of Portugal:

1	Minho	6	Beira Baixa
2	Douro	7	Estremadura
3	Trás-os-Montes	8	Ribatejo
4	Beira Alta	9	Alentejo
5	Beira Litoral	10	Algarve

And some main cities:

1	Lisboa	6	Porto
2	Faro	7	Braga
3	Guarda	8	Évora
4	Setúbal	9	Portalegre
5	Coimbra	10	Vila Real

1
MUITO PRAZER
Pleased to meet you

In this unit you will learn

- basic greetings
- how to ask and say how people are
- how to ask and give names
- common courtesies

Antes de começar
Before you begin

 Make sure you have read the Introduction to the course and understood the tips for learning, which give you useful advice on how to make the most of this course. If you have the cassette, use it as much as you can, as it will help your progress considerably. Repeat phrases often, using the pause button on your cassette player to give you time to work at your own speed.

Actividade

If you have visited Portugal, either on holiday or business, you may well have heard some basic greetings, and may even have used some yourself. Try to think of a few words now and say them aloud, then check with the following list to see how you've got on – you probably know several.

Bom dia.	*Good morning, hello.*
Boa tarde.	*Good afternoon, hello.*
Boa noite.	*Good evening (night), hello.*
Olá.	*Hi. (Hello.)*
Até logo.	*See you later.*
Até já.	*See you soon.*
Até amanhã.	*See you tomorrow.*
Até a próxima.	*See you next time.*
Tchau.	*Bye for now.*
Adeus.	*Goodbye.*

Comentário Commentary

Portuguese greetings are less fixed to the time of day than the corresponding English phrases. **Bom dia** is used up until around 1.00 p.m., when many businesses close for lunch. **Boa tarde** is used during the afternoon and into the early evening. You will soon get an idea of when to use each greeting listening to Portuguese people during their day-to-day routines. The first three expressions above are also used as goodbye and are often accompanied by **adeus**, eg. **adeus boa noite** and so on. **Tchau** is imported from Brazilian soap operas; it is very casual, as is **olá** and **olá bom dia**.

 ———— ## Diálogo 1 *Dialogue 1* ————

Paula meets a neighbour and briefly greets him.

Paula	**Bom dia senhor Mendes. Como está?**
Sr. Mendes	**Estou bem, obrigado, e a senhora?**
Paula	**Bem obrigada.**

Paula sees an acquaintance, Ana, approaching.

Paula	**Olá Ana, está boa?**
Ana	**Estou, e a Paula?**
Paula	**Também, estou, obrigada.**
Ana	**Então, até já.**
Paula	**Adeus, até logo.**

como está? *how are you?*	**e** *and*
estou bem *I'm well*	**também** *also*
obrigado *thank you (by males)*	**obrigada** *thank you (by females)*
está boa? *are you well?*	**então** *well then/right then*
(*to a woman*)	

 —————— **Para estudar** ——————

1 Obrigado/obrigada

In this first dialogue you met **obrigado** and **obrigada**, both meaning *thank you*. **Obrigado** is used by men and **obrigada** by women: these are the masculine and feminine forms of the same word.

Many words in Portuguese are divided into male and female forms; this comes from Latin, the base of the Portuguese language. If you know a bit of any other Latin-based language, such as French, this concept will not be new to you. If you don't, don't worry there will be plenty of opportunities to get used to the two versions of the same word. In Portuguese, the ending of words shows whether that word is masculine (usually an **-o** ending), or feminine (usually **-a**). You will learn more about this as you go along.

2 You

The Portuguese use a different word for *you* depending on how well they know the person, whether the person is in a higher social position, has senior work status, if they are older, and so on. In the dialogue you met two of the more formal words meaning *you*.

o senhor (male)	*you* lit. *the gentleman / sir*
a senhora (female)	*you* lit. *the lady*

The other *you* you have met is **o** or **a** + the name of the person:

o Miguel	*you* (*to Miguel*, masculine)
a Paula	*you* (*to Paula*, feminine)

This is often used between colleagues or by older people to younger people.

You will learn more of these varied forms as you go along.

3 I am, you are: to be

In the dialogue, people were asking and saying how they are, using:

estou	*I am*
está	*you are*

In English, *to be* is the infinitive of the verb (this is the form of the verb you will find in a dictionary). In Portuguese the equivalent infinitive is **estar**.

The verb **estar**, *to be*, is used to describe temporary feelings, states, characteristics and places.

4 Questions

In Portuguese, you can ask a simple question by raising your voice at the end of a sentence. There is no change in word-order, as is often the case in English questions.

Como está?	*How are you?* (lit. *how you are?*)
Está boa?	*Are you well?* (lit. *you are well?*)

Actividades

1   Fill in the gaps in this dialogue.

Ana   **Boa noite senhor Silva. Como . . . . . ?**
Sr. Silva   **. . . . . bem, obrigado. E a senhora?**
Ana   **Estou . . . , ...**
Sr. Silva   **Então, boa . . . . . e . . . amanhã.**
Ana   **. . . noite.**

2   What would you say to these people in the following situations?

   (*a*)   meeting your friend Ana Paula at mid-morning
   (*b*)   bumping into a business colleague at lunch time
   (*c*)   leaving a group of friends mid-afternoon – and you'll be seeing them again tomorrow
   (*d*)   popping into town to go shopping – you'll see your family later
   (*e*)   meeting your teacher in the evening

3 You have just met Nuno in the street. Complete your conversation in Portuguese following the English prompts.

	Nuno	**Boa tarde, como está?**
(a)	You	*Say hello. Tell him you're fine, thanks. Ask him how he is.*
	Nuno	**Estou bem, obrigado.**
(b)	You	*Say goodbye. Tell him you'll see him tomorrow.*
	Nuno	**Então, até a próxima.**

Documento número 1

At what part of the day is this programme aired?

> **TARDE DE CINEMA:**
> **"O ÚLTIMO COMBOIO**
> **DE GUN HILL"**
> O filme em exibição foi realizado por John Sturges e conta com Kirk Douglas e Anthony Quinn nos principais papéis. *[2696442]*

Diálogo 2 *Dialogue 2*

Nuno takes Paula to a party, where she meets some people she doesn't know.

Nuno	**Boa noite Miguel, estás bom?**
Miguel	**Estou, e tu?**
Nuno	**Estou óptimo, obrigado.**
Miguel	*(turning to Paula)* **Desculpa, como te chamas?**
Paula	**Chamo-me Paula, e tu?**
Miguel	**Miguel.**
Paula	**Muito prazer**
Miguel	**Igualmente**

desculpa	*excuse me*	**estou óptimo/a**	*I'm really well/fine*
chamo-me	*I am called/ my name is*	**muito prazer**	*pleased to meet you*
estás bom?	*are you well?*	**igualmente**	*likewise*
(*to a man*)			

Comentário Commentary

The Portuguese, although more reserved than the Spanish, are generally more tactile than the English; it is common when you greet someone to shake hands, slap each other's backs, or kiss on each cheek – although this has become a fashionable peck on one cheek only in some places. Obviously if you are meeting people for the first time take your cue from their behaviour towards you – if you are too informal you may offend.

 —————————— **Para estudar** ——————————

1 Informal you

In dialogue 2, the friends addressed each other by **tu**, which is the informal form of *you* – for friends, family and young people. The verb form also changed from **está** to **estás**.

está	*you are* (more formal)
estás	*you are* (informal)

2 Chamo-me . . . My name is . . .

You will have noticed that when Paula was asked **Como *te* chamas?**, she responded with **chamo-*me***. Don't worry at this stage about the varied position of the words **te** and **me**. Note that when asking the name of someone older, or whom you do not know very well, you use **como *se* chama?**, which is more formal.

3 Desculpa Excuse me

The word **desculpa** (or **desculpe** when used with strangers) can be used to mean *I'm sorry* in situations such as in dialogue 2, as well as when interrupting a conversation, on approaching someone in the street to ask a question, or for apologising if you have bumped into someone. You will also hear:

perdão	*sorry / I beg your pardon*
com licença	*excuse me* (if you want to pass by)

Possible responses include:

não faz mal	*don't worry*
com certeza/faz favor	*of course / go ahead*

Actividades

4 What would you say to these people to find out their names?

(a) Ana Maria (b) José (c) Senhor Mendes

5 The following dialogue has become mixed-up. Can you unscramble it? To help you get started the first line is **Bom dia, como está?**

Lúcia	**Bem obrigada.**
Sr. Silva	**Eduardo.**
Lúcia	**Bom dia, como está?**
Lúcia	**Chamo-me Lúcia, e o senhor?**
Sr. Silva	**Estou bem, obrigado, e a senhora?**
Sr. Silva	**Igualmente.**
Lúcia	**Muito prazer.**
Sr. Silva	**Desculpe, mas como se chama?**

6 The expressions for six greetings (*hello*/*goodbye*) are hidden in this wordsearch. The words run across, down, up, backwards and diagonally.

K	O	B	D	L	G	S	E
M	T	A	Z	P	O	D	O
A	S	J	D	H	R	W	F
I	L	E	N	A	P	J	C
D	A	T	T	D	O	R	Q
M	J	A	F	E	A	Z	S
O	O	R	K	U	B	C	Y
B	S	C	T	S	E	F	P
O	G	O	L	E	T	A	D
C	T	S	B	R	O	L	A

Parabéns! (*Well done!*) You have completed the first unit. Now try this **Avaliação** to see what you have learnt.

Avaliação

Now check you can:

(*a*) say good afternoon and ask someone (formally) how they are.
(*b*) say goodnight and 'see you next time'.
(*c*) ask someone their name (informally).
(*d*) give your name.
(*e*) apologise for stepping on someone's foot!
(*f*) say you're pleased to meet someone.

2
DE ONDE É

Where are you from?

In this unit you will learn

- how to ask where people are from
- how to say where you are from
- how to talk about nationalities

--- **Antes de começar** ---

Different people have different ways of learning but most people would agree that studying for 20 minutes regularly is better than occasionally spending two hours in one go. Listen to the dialogues once or twice without the book (or read them aloud if you haven't got the cassette). Then go through the new words one by one.

--- **Diálogo 1** ---

A group of people have just met at a party. They are finding out where each other comes from.

Sr. Pereira **Boa noite. Chamo-me Rui Pereira. E como se chama a senhora?**

Julia **Julia.**

Sr. Pereira **Muito prazer, Julia. De onde é?**

Julia **Sou inglesa; sou de Londres. E o senhor de onde é?**

Sr. Pereira **Sou português, sou de Lisboa.**

de onde é? *where are you from?*	**Londres** *London*
sou *I am*	**português** *Portuguese (man)*
inglesa *English (woman)*	**Lisboa** *Lisbon*
sou de *I am from*	

Diálogo 2

Senhor Pereira asks a couple where they come from.

Sr. Pereira	**Boa noite. De onde são os senhores?**
Susana	**Somos da Espanha. Somos espanhois.**
Mário	**A Susana é de Madrid, e eu sou de Barcelona. E o senhor, de onde é?**
Sr. Pereira	**Pois, sou de Portugal!**

de onde são? *where are you from?*	**espanhois** *Spanish (people)*
os senhores *you (polite, plural form)*	**é** *is*
somos *we are*	**eu** *I*
Espanha *Spain*	**pois** *well*

Para estudar

1 *More of* to be

In the previous unit, you learned **está** *you are* and **estou** *I am*, to talk about how people are feeling. These dialogues introduce you to another Portuguese verb **ser** *to be*; it is generally used to describe more permanent characteristics, such as your nationality and where you come from.

Sou de Portugal.	*I am from Portugal.*
De onde **é**?	*Where **are you** from?*
Susana **é** de Madrid.	*Susan **is** from Madrid.*
Somos da Espanha.	*We are from Spain.*
De onde **são**?	*Where **are you** (pl) from?*

2 I, you, he, she, we *and so on*

This set of words (personal pronouns) indicates who is *in play* at any time, and who is the subject of the verb. But these words are rarely used in Portuguese, because the ending of the verb (the action word) shows the person in question:

sou	*I am*
eu sou	*I am*

The personal pronoun is useful for giving emphasis (*I'm from Spain*), or when a particular verb ending may indicate one of a choice of people (é = *you **are**, she/he/it* **is**). You will learn more about verbs later.

3 Nationality

In unit 1 you learnt that certain words in Portuguese have either a masculine or feminine ending, depending on who (or what) that word is referring to. The same is true of words describing people's nationality. Also, if you are talking about more than one person, you must remember to change the word into a plural one. This sounds rather complex, but in fact, once you have got used to the idea, it is very logical, and with practice it becomes second nature.

Have a look at this table and compare the singular and plural forms of the nationalities:

	masculine singular	feminine singular	masculine plural	feminine plural
A Inglaterra *England*	inglês	inglesa	ingleses	inglesas
Portugal *Portugal*	português	portuguesa	portugueses	portuguesas
Os Estados Unidos *U.S.A.*	americano	americana	americanos	americanas
A Itália *Italy*	italiano	italiana	italianos	italianas
A Escócia *Scotland*	escocês	escocesa	escoceses	escocesas
A Alemanha *Germany*	alemão	alemã	alemães	alemãs
O Brasil *Brazil*	brasileiro	brasileira	brasileiros	brasileiras

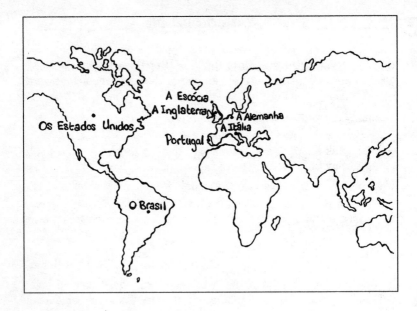

If you have two or more males, you will use the masculine plural, similarly, a group of women will need the feminine plural. However, should you have a mixed group, the masculine plural is applied, even if your group consists of 100 women and just one man!

Notice that the names of countries can be masculine or feminine, and the endings reflect this. Some countries, such as Portugal itself, do not use this structure. This is just an anomaly in the language – you have to get used to them! The U.S.A, is plural (**os**), as it refers to the group of states.

O Brasil	(*Brazil*)
A Itália	(*Italy*)
Os Estados Unidos	(*United States*)
Sou alemã	*I am German* (f.)
Falo inglês	*I speak English*
Tom é escocês	*Tom is Scottish*

Actividades

1 Check with the nationalities table on page 19 and do the following:

   (a) Say which country you are from.
   (b) Give your nationality.
   (c) Ask Senhor Silva where he's from.
   (d) Say that Ana is Brazilian.
   (e) Ask Mr. and Mrs. Brito where they are from.
   (f) Say that Paulo is from Italy.
   (g) Say that the McDonalds are Scottish.

2 Fill in the spaces in the speech bubbles of the following people, who are talking about their nationalities and where they are from.

Maria

O sr/a sra. Schmidt

3 Now write sentences about the same people (*a*), (*b*), (*c*), (*d*), (*e*), (*f*), using the correct part of **ser** (*to be*). It is common practice in Portugal to use **o** (masculine) **a** (feminine) before people's names, hence the first example would read:

A Maria **é** de Portugal. *Maria is from Portugal.*
  É portuguesa. *She is Portuguese.*

You could use the word for *she* (**ela**) here, to emphasise the sentence.

Ela é portuguesa.

Now try the rest. You could use *he* (**ele**) and *they* (**eles** masculine, **elas** feminine).

Diálogo 3

David has just met someone and he is trying to start a conversation.

David	**Bom dia. Desculpe, mas fala inglês?**
João	**Não, não falo. O senhor é inglês?**
David	**Sim, sou. Falo um pouco de português. Mas, o senhor é português?**
João	**Não, não sou.**
David	**Mas fala bem português.**
João	**Sou brasileiro!**

mas	*but*	**falo**	*I speak*
fala . . .?	*do you speak . . . ?*	**um pouco de**	*a bit of*
não	*no/not*	**bem**	*well*
sim	*yes*		

Para estudar

1 *Sim and não*/yes and no

To say something negative, you place the word **não** before the verb:

não sou.	*I am not*
não falo.	*I do not speak*

Note there is no Portuguese equivalent of the word *do* in this kind of sentence. On answering a question, the Portuguese tend to use a double negative, as in the dialogue: **não, não falo no**, *I do **not** speak*.

The word for *yes* is **sim**. Both of these words are nasalised – i.e. they should be pronounced like many French words, at the back of the nose. This takes some practice for English speakers, so keep trying! See the Pronunciation Guide ➡️ **P.** 5 for more on this.

2 Languages

The name of a language is the same as the male nationality, hence **italiano** can mean the *Italian language*, or an *Italian man*. A German woman could say:

Sou alemã, falo alemão.	*I'm German (a German woman),*
	I speak German.

Comentário

As Portuguese is a language spoken in many continents, from South America, across Africa, and into Asia, as well as in Continental Portugal (including Madeira and the Azores), you may well meet various speakers of the language on your travels. Brazil, of course, has an enormous number of Portuguese speakers, and Brazilian soap operas are extremely popular in Portugal. The differences between Brazilian and European Portuguese are roughly akin to those between American and British English on pronunciation, vocabulary, and some points of grammar. In Dialogue 3 ➡️ **P.** 23 João was Brazilian. Did you notice his different accent?

——————— **Actividades** ———————

4 How would you do the following:

   (*a*) Ask someone if they speak Italian.
   (*b*) Say you are not American.
   (*c*) Say you speak Portuguese and English.
   (*d*) Ask someone if they speak Portuguese.
   (*e*) Say you are not German, but you speak German.

Veradeiro ou falso

5 Decide whether these statements about which languages people speak is true (V=**veradeiro**) or false (F=**falso**). Assume each one only speaks their own language!

   (*a*) A Sara é dos Estados Unidos. Fala alemão.
   (*b*) O Marco fala italiano; é da Itália.
   (*c*) Eu sou do Brasil, falo português.
   (*d*) A senhora Gomes é da Escócia. Fala inglês.
   (*e*) O senhor Mendes fala alemão. É português.

Documento número 2a:

   (*a*) Which language is the most widely spoken?
   (*b*) Which are the last two on the table?

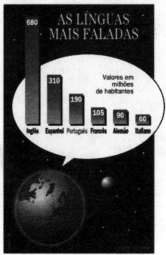

Aqui fala-se . . .

6 An interviewer (**entrevistador**) is doing a questionnaire about languages and nationalities. You decide to participate. Follow the prompts to help you complete the dialogue.

Entrevistador **Boa tarde. Desculpe, mas fala português?**
(a) You *Say yes, you speak a little bit.*
Entrevistador **É da Alemanha?**
(b) You *Say no, you're not German, and give your nationality.*
Entrevistador **Entâo** (well then)**, fala inglês?**
(c) You *Say yes, you speak English, and also Italian.*
Entrevistador **Fala bem português.**
(d) You *Say thank you, and goodbye.*

Documento número 2b

Which languages are spoken at this shop?

AQUI FALAM-SE
INGLÊS,
PORTUGUÊS,
ALEMÃO

Avaliação

(a) Ask Paulo where he's from.
(b) Say which country you are from.
(c) Ask Senhor Mendes if he is Brazilian.
(d) Ask where the Senhores Oliveira come from.
(e) Speak on behalf of yourself and a friend, giving your nationality.
(f) Say that Julia is Portuguese.
(g) Ask if João is from the U.S.A.
(h) Ask someone if they speak English.
(i) Say no, you don't speak German.
(j) Say yes, you are English.

3
ONDE MORA?
Where do you live?

In this unit you will learn

- how to talk about where you live
- how to talk about addresses
- how to talk about where you work
- how to ask other people about where they live and work
- numbers 0–20

Antes de começar

There is a variety of situations in which you may have to talk about where people live; it could be an informal conversation, or you may be filling in forms (at the bank, for example), or you may need someone's address in order to pay them a visit. There are, in fact, two verbs in Portuguese, which can be used to mean to live: **morar** and **viver**. **Morar** has close associations with **morada** meaning address, and **viver** used to be on a larger scale, such as one's country, but, nowadays, you will hear both verbs equally. The dialogues in this unit will give you examples in each verb.

Diálogo 1

Ana is finding out where different people live. Listen to the dialogue then follow it in the book.

Ana	**Boa noite senhor Mendes. Onde mora?**
Sr. Mendes	**Moro em Lisboa, na avenida da República. E a Ana, mora em Lisboa?**
Ana	**Não, moro aqui em Albufeira. Onde moram os senhores Silva?**
Sr. Mendes	**Moram no Porto, na praça São Vicente. Onde mora o José?**
Ana	**O José? Pois, agora vive no Brasil.**

mora *you live, he, she lives*	**aqui** *here*
moro *I live*	**moram** *they live, you* (pl) *live*
em *in*	**(a) praça** *(the) square*
na *on/in (the)*	**agora** *now*
(a) avenida *(the) avenue*	**vive** *he/she lives, you live*
a avenida da República *(the) Republic Avenue*	

 —————— **Para estudar** ——————

1 *o, a* the

You have already learnt about the idea of masculine and feminine words, and you have seen the words **o** and **a** (yes, they may be only one letter, but they are in fact words!) used with certain countries, and with people's names. In the dialogue above, there are examples of these words used to describe where people live:

| a avenida | *the avenue* |
| a praça | *the square* |

Everything – that is all objects – in the Portuguese language are either masculine or feminine. Most masculine words end in **-o**, and most feminine ones, like the examples above, end in **-a**. Likewise the words for *the* are **o** for masculine words, and **a** for feminine words. As you progress you will find many words do not fit the **-o/-a** ending structure, so you will have to learn from the vocabulary box which group they belong to. To form the plural *the*, (i.e. when talking about more than one object) just add an **-s** to the appropriate form.

Wherever helpful words will be identified with the **o** or **a**, or (m) or (f) in the vocabulary boxes in the rest of this course.

as avenidas   *the squares*

2 *Em* in/on

The word for describing *in* or *on*, is **em**, as seen in **moro *em* Lisboa**. However, when you follow this word by any of the words for *the*, the words join together; usually when this happens, it is to help pronunciation, as some combinations of sounds would otherwise be rather awkward. So, the combinations, or contractions, are as follows:

- em + o/a   = no/na
  in + the (masculine/feminine)   = *in / on the*

  em + a praça
  na praça   = *in the square*

and in the plural,

- em + os/as   = nos, nas
  em + as avenidas
  nas avenidas   = *in the avenues*

3 Forming verbs

Up to now, you have been using parts of the two verbs **ser/estar** *to be* to talk about different aspects of people. You learnt in unit 2 how to use the verb **falar** *to speak* and now you have been introduced to the verbs **morar/viver** *to live*. Many verbs follow the same pattern of endings as **falar**, as the **-ar** ending is the most common in Portuguese. Compare **falar**, **morar** and **trabalhar** (*to work*) which you will use later in this chapter:

falar *to speak*		**morar** *to live*	
fal**o**	I speak	mor**o**	I live
fal**a**	he, she speaks/you speak	mor**a**	he, she lives/you live
fal**amos**	we speak	mor**amos**	we live
fal**am**	they speak/you (pl) speak	mor**am**	they live/you (pl) live

---

trabalhar *to work*

trabalho   I work
trabalha   he, she works/you work
trabalhamos we work
trabalham   they work/you (pl) work

Can you spot the similar patterns? It is the continued presence of the letter **a**, brought down from the initial **-ar** ending.

Verbs are a complex part of any language, so you will need to take your time to get used to them. Don't worry if you get things wrong to begin with, the important thing is to have a go.

 ——————————— **Actividades** ———————————

1 So, now have a go. How do you do the following:

    (*a*) Ask senhora Gomes where she lives.
    (*b*) Say that you live in England.
    (*c*) Say that Maria lives in the square.
    (*d*) Ask where the senhores Neto live.
    (*e*) Ask Renato if he lives in Germany.

2 Match up the people on the left with a correct part of the verb **morar** and the correct part of **no/na** *in/on the* to fit the place they live.

Eu (*I*)—moro   no   praça
        mora   na
        moram nos
              nas

(*a*)	Lúcia (*she*)	moramos	___	avenida.
(*b*)	Nós (*we*)	mora	no	rua (*street*).
(*c*)	(*you*)	moro	na	beco (*alley*).
(*d*)	Eles (*they*)	moram	___	praça.

Leitura

Listen to and follow the passage below, in which João is giving his address to someone, and describing exactly where he lives.

Moro em Silves no Algarve, na rua Samora Barros, número seis, e o apartamento fica no terceiro andar, à esquerda.

Now listen to and read about where Marília lives:

Eu vivo em Portugal, em Lisboa. Vivo numa casa antiga na praça de Camões, número quinze, segundo andar, à direita.

(o) número *number*	**à esquerda** *on the left*
o apartamento *the apartment, flat*	**numa casa antiga** *in an old house*
fica *is situated*	**(o) segundo** *second*
(o) terceiro *third*	**à direita** *on the right*
(o) andar *floor*	

Para estudar

1 *Os números* numbers

You cannot get very far without numbers, in any language, as they creep into so many daily transactions – addresses, time, money, quantities – so you must start now to build up a good grasp of them. Let's start with 0–20. Listen to the numbers and repeat them aloud before you look at them. Say them every day for at least a week, and test yourself by counting backwards, or asking someone to test you out aloud.

0	zero	11	onze
1	um, uma	12	doze
2	dois, duas	13	treze
3	três	14	catorze
4	quatro	15	quinze
5	cinco	16	dezasseis
6	seis	17	dezassete
7	sete	18	dezoito
8	oito	19	dezanove
9	nove	20	vinte
10	dez		

Numbers *one* and *two* have both a masculine and a feminine form – so if you are talking about two houses, **duas** cas**as**.

2 1st, 2nd, 3rd and so on

primeiro	1st
segundo	2nd
terceiro	3rd
quarto	4th
quinto	5th

You will learn further ones as you go along. If you are talking about anything feminine, then the final **-o** must change to an **-a**:

a terceir**a** cas**a**   *the third house*

These words are not only used for talking about floors in a building, you will also find them in unit 11 on directions, and unit 7 on days of the week.

3 *Um, uma* a, an

The words for number *one* are also the masculine and feminine forms of the words for *a* (*an*). Therefore, you can talk in terms of **uma casa** *a house* or **um apartamento** *an apartment*. Remember always to check in the vocabulary lists to see whether the word is masculine or feminine. This is referred to as the word's gender. If you are using a dictionary, then the word will usually be followed by (m) or (f). If there is no indication of gender, it is because the word belongs to the standard **-o/-a** ending.

4 *Num/numa* in a/on a

In the reading, you came across the expression **vivo *numa* casa antiga** (*I live in an old house*). This is another example of a contracted structure, just like the **no/na** you learnt in unit 2. Here you have: **em** + **um/uma**, becoming **num** and **numa**. Again, it makes it easier to say: try saying **em um** – it sticks in your nose area and is very awkward.

5 *uma casa antiga* an old house

Words that describe things (adjectives), such as **antigo** (*old*) are usually placed after the word they are describing. They also have to have the same appropriate masculine or feminine ending, and must be either singular or plural. This is called agreeing. Therefore a modern apartment would be **um apartamento moderno**, and two old houses would be **duas casas antigas**. You will learn more of these words in the next unit.

 ———————— **Actividades** ————————

3 The following people have got lost. Look at the descriptions they give of where they live, and match them up with the address plates:

a.

Praça de S.Jorge
Nº 6

(i) Moro num apartamento moderno numa praça. Fica no terceiro andar, à direita

b.

Rua do Ouro
Nº 11

(ii) Moro na Rua do Ouro, número dezasseis, segundo andar.

c.

PRAÇA
LISBOA 56
3 DIR

(iii) Moro na Praça de São Jorge numa casa moderna, número seis.

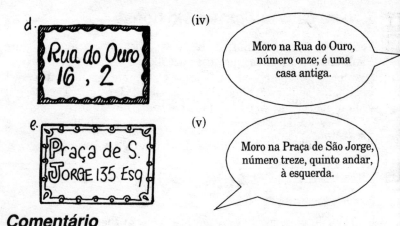

d.

Rua do Ouro
16 , 2

(iv)

Moro na Rua do Ouro,
número onze; é uma
casa antiga.

e.

Praça de S.
Jorge 135 Esq

(v)

Moro na Praça de São Jorge,
número treze, quinto andar,
à esquerda.

Comentário

You may have noticed an abbreviation on the address plates above, regarding the number of the floor people live on – 3°, 2° and so on meaning third, second. Other common address abbreviations to look out for are R. (rua), r/c (rés-do-chão = *ground floor*), Av. (avenida), Pr. (praça), esq. (esquerda), dir. (direita). Many streets are named after famous historical or military heroes, or dates of historical events, such as 25 de Abril (*25th April* – when the 1974 revolution took place), or Praça de Camões (named after Portugal's national poet).

Documento número 3

Look at the two address cards and decide which place belongs to senhor Mendes, whose establishment is on the ground floor, on a street.

Pastelaria Snack Bar

ANTIQUA

Aberto das 7:30 às 21:30h. Encerra ao Sábado.
Rua Dr. Augusto E. Nunes, 40 r/c • Tel. 29698

Café-Restaurante **O AVENIDA**

• Cozinha Regional
• Petiscos
• Com nova sala de refeições

Aberto das 7 às 23h. Encerra aos Domingos.

Av. São Sebastião, 25 • Tel. 33872

——— Diálogo 2 ———

Paulo and Maria are talking about where they work.

Paulo   **Maria, onde é que trabalha?**
Maria   **Trabalho em Faro, no aeroporto.**
Paulo   **E o que faz?**
Maria   **Sou Controladora de tráfego aéreo. E o Paulo, onde trabalha?**
Paulo   **Sou bancário; trabalho num banco em Tavira.**

onde trabalha? *where do you work?*	**trabalho** *I work*
onde é que trabalha? *where is it that you work?*	**o que faz?** *what do you do?*

Now, could you work out where they work? Have a look again at what they say, and see if you can find any connections with English words. Maria works at Faro airport, as an air traffic controller, and Paulo is a bank clerk in a bank in Tavira.

——— Para estudar ———

1 *onde (é que) . . . ?* where (is it that) . . . ?

You will often hear Portuguese people inserting the expression **é que** into questions, usually to pad out a bit what they are saying. So you could say **onde é que mora? (onde mora?)** as well as **onde é que trabalha? (onde trabalha?)**

2 Professions

When someone asks you **onde trabalha?**, or **o que faz?**, there are two ways you can answer, as Maria did in the dialogue. You can either say **trabalho em . . .** *I work in* or **sou . . .** *I am . . .* When you are describing your place of work, don't forget the contractions **num**, **numa**, **no** and **na**.

So, you could say:

Trabalho num banco	*I work in a bank*
Trabalho numa escola	*in a school*
Trabalho num escritório	*in an office*
Trabalho numa empresa	*in a business*
Trabalho na universidade	*in the university*
Trabalho no banco Espírito Santo	*in the Espírito Santo bank*

Or,

Sou professor/professora	*I am a teacher*
Sou estudante/estudante	*student*
Sou escritor/escritora	*writer*
Sou médico/médica	*doctor*
Sou enfermeiro/enfermeira	*nurse*
Sou advogado/advogada	*lawyer*

You may be a **dona de casa** (*housewife*) or a **homem/mulher de negócios** (*businessman / woman*), or you may not work, **não trabalho**, **estou reformado/a** (*I do not work, I'm retired*) **estou desempregado/a** (*I'm unemployed*).

✳ With names of professions, Portuguese do not use the word *a*, they say literally *I am teacher*.

 ———————— **Actividades** ————————

4 Try these.

   (*a*) Ask senhor Gomes where he works.
   (*b*) Say that you are a student.
   (*c*) Ask José what he does for a living.
   (*d*) Say where you work.
   (*e*) Say that you do not work.

5 Work out where these people work and fill in the locations in the grid.

   (*a*) Sou estudante
   (*b*) Sou bancário
   (*c*) Sou mulher de negócios
   (*d*) Sou controlador de tráfego aéreo
   (*e*) Sou secretária
   (*f*) Sou professora.

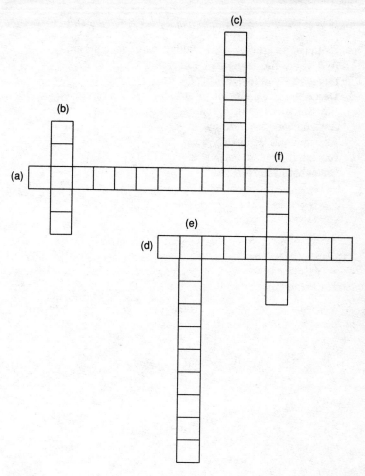

6 Complete the sums, choosing from the words in the list on the right-hand side.

(a) Dois + três   = ___ treze
(b) Vinte – oito   = ___ dezanove
(c) Dezassete – quatro   = ___ dezoito
(d) Nove + nove   = ___ cinco
(e) Dez – oito   = ___ dois
(f) Quinze + quatro   = ___ doze

Avaliação

Check if you can now do the following:

(*a*) Count up to 20, forwards and backwards – out loud.
(*b*) Ask where the senhores Pereira live.
(*c*) Say where you live.
(*d*) Describe the location of your house.
(*e*) Say that you live in a modern house.
(*f*) Ask someone where they work.
(*g*) Ask someone what they do.
(*h*) Say what your profession is.
(*i*) Say where you work.

4
A FAMÍLIA
The family

In this unit you will learn

- how to point people out
- how to describe your family
- how to talk about age

Antes de começar

Before learning a second verb meaning *to be* in this unit, look back at unit 2 to make sure you can say *I am* and *you are*.

—————— Diálogo 1 ——————

Senhor Moura is pointing out his family to a friend while at a party.

Alexandra	**Boa tarde Senhor Moura. Está cá sozinho?**
Sr. Moura	**Não, estou com a minha família. Este é o meu filho Roberto, e esta é a minha filha mais velha, Sonia.**
Alexandra	**Muito prazer. E a senhora Moura?**
Sr. Moura	**Pois, a minha mulher é aquela senhora ali.**
Alexandra	**E quem é aquele senhor ali?**
Sr. Mouro	**É o nosso chefe!**

cá *here*		**mais velha** *eldest*
sozinho *alone*		**a minha mulher** *my wife*
com *with*		**aquela (f)** *that*
a minha família *my family*		**lá, ali** *there, over there*
este (m) *this*		**quem?** *who?*
o meu filho *my son*		**aquele (m)** *that*
esta (f) *this*		**o nosso chefe** *our boss*
a minha filha *my daughter*		

Comentário

There are two words for *wife* in Portuguese; **a (minha) mulher**, as in the dialogue, and also **a esposa**. The latter seems to be considered more polite, if you were asking after someone's wife, **como está a sua esposa?**, and the former tends to be used more when talking about one's own wife. When in doubt, take your cue from what Portuguese people are saying around you as expressions, like fashions, come and go.

Para estudar

1 Este/aquele this/that

You should have noticed the different words used in the dialogue for pointing out people. **Este** (m)/**esta** (f) is used for people, or things near to you, and **aquele** (m)/**aquela** (f) for those at a distance. To talk about more than one person or thing, just add an **-s**, to make the plurals *these* and *those*.

este	esta	estes	estas	*this/these*
aquele	aquela	aqueles	aquelas	*that/those*

aquelas senhoras	*those women*
estes senhores	*these men*

2   *O meu/o nosso* my/our

When talking about a possession (this includes family members) you must make sure that the word you use for *my*, *your* and so on agrees with the object in possession. This can sometimes be awkward to grasp, but when you remember that these words are describing the possession in some way, then you have already learnt in unit 2 that descriptive words (adjectives) agree with the word they are describing. Even though you may be a man talking about your daughter, you would use the feminine word for *my*. Here are some of the possessive words you are going to need:

	masculine word	feminine word
my	o meu	a minha
your (singular)	o seu	a sua
our	o nosso	a nossa

To talk about more than one possessed object (i.e. in the plural), add an **-s** to the appropriate word.

as nossas filhas   *our daughters*

Did you notice in each case the word for the (**o, a, os, as**) is included? So what you actually end up saying is *the my*, and so on. This is just a quirk of the language – don't worry, all languages are full of them!

3   *Mais ou menos* more or less

When describing someone who is older, younger, taller, smaller, etc. you need the words **mais** (*more*) and **menos** (*less*) used with the appropriate adjective. So you can have combinations such as:

mais velho	*older*	o mais velho	*the oldest*
mais novo	*younger*	o mais novo	*the youngest*
mais alto	*taller*	o mais alto	*the tallest*
menos alto mais baixo }	*shorter*	o mais baixo	*the shortest*

Don't forget to make the adjectives agree. A girl who is younger will be **mais nova**, and boys who are the tallest will be **os mais altos**. The words should appear after the person or thing they refer to:

o filho mais alto   *the tallest son*

———————— **Actividades** ————————

1   Use the box of family members to help you complete these sentences following the guide in brackets.

o filho *son*	**o irmão** *brother*
a filha *daughter*	**a irmã** *sister*
o marido *husband*	**o pai** *father*
a mulher *wife*	**a mãe** *mother*

The plural of **filho** – **filhos**, can mean sons, or children.

(a) Este é (*my brother*) _____ .
(b) Aquela é (*our mother*) _____ .
(c) Esta é (*your daughter*) _____ .
(d) Estes são (*our sons*) _____ .
(e) Aquele é (*my father*) _____ .

2   How would you say the following:

(a) Ana is the youngest daughter.
(b) Miguel is our tallest brother.
(c) They are my older sons.
(d) António is shorter.
(e) Maria and Paula are taller.

 ———————— **Leitura** ————————

Listen to senhor Moura describing his family, then read the passage a couple of times to make sure you have understood it.

Tenho uma família bastante pequena. A minha mulher chama-se Rosa e é professora. Trabalha numa escola secundária em Braga. Ela é muito simpática e elegante. Temos três filhos: a Sonia, que é a filha mais velha, e a Catarina, a irmã, e o Roberto, o filho mais novo. A Sonia trabalha num hospital, e os outros dois são estudantes. O Roberto é alto e desportivo, e a Catarina é muito calma.

tenho *I have*	**simpática** *nice*
bastante *quite*	**elegante** *elegant*
pequena *small*	**emos** *we have*
escola secundária *secondary/*	**ﬁ outros** *the other(s)*
high school	**uesportivo** *sporty*
muito *very*	**calma** *calm, easy-going*

Actividades

3 Now answer these questions about the família Moura.

   (a) Como se chama a esposa do (*of*) senhor Moura?
   (b) Onde é que ela trabalha?
   (c) Quem é o filho mais novo?
   (d) Como é a Catarina? (*What is she like?*)
   (e) O que faz a Sonia?
   (f) O Roberto é baixo?

Para estudar

1 Ter to have

This is an important verb for you to learn, as you will be using it again later in the book. The main parts you need to know are:

ter *to have*	
tenho	I have
tem	you (singular) have, he/she/it has
temos	we have
têm	you (pl) have, they have

2 Describing people

Senhor Moura described his family, using adjectives to tell you about their characteristics. He used the words **simpático** (*nice*), **elegante** (*elegant*), **desportivo** (*sporty*), and **calmo** (*calm*). There are many words you can use to describe people. Here are a few more suggestions: remember to make the words agree with the person you are describing, by changing final **-os** (m. pl), to **-as** (f. pl).

solitário/a	*lonely*	**barulhento/a**	*noisy*	
nervoso/a	*nervous*	**orgulhoso/a**	*proud*	
sério/a	*serious*	**charmoso/a, encantador/a**	*charming*	
trabalhador(a)	*industrious*	**artístico/a**	*artistic*	
preguiçoso/a	*lazy*	**honesto/a**	*honest*	

3 *Ser* or *estar* to be *or* to be

Do you remember, in units 1 and 2, the two ways of expressing *I am*, etc. in Portuguese? One is using the verb **ser** (for more permanent characteristics) and the other with the verb **estar** (when situations are more temporary). In the **Leitura**, senhor Moura described the characteristics of his family members using **ser**, but if he had wanted to say how someone was at the moment, he would have used **estar**. To see how this works compare these two phrases:

Ela é calma.   *She is calm*
                   (i.e. a calm person, always).

Ela está calma.   *She's calm* (at the moment).

It's important to think carefully before you use these verbs, but you'll get lots of practice as you progress through this course. Let's just check you know the parts of the two:

Ser		Estar	
sou	I am	**estou**	I am
é	you are, he/she is	**está**	you are, he/she is
somos	we are	**estamos**	we are
são	you (pl) are, they are	**estão**	you (pl) are, they are

Actividades

4 How would you say the following in Portuguese?

(a) Do you (sing) have a daughter?
(b) We have two children.
(c) Does she have a brother?
(d) I have a sister.
(e) Do you (pl) have children?

5 Find eight words in the wordsearch, which describe people's characteristics. The words may run up, down, diagonally, backwards or forwards.

P	R	E	G	U	I	Ç	O	S	O
A	T	C	L	I	A	T	I	T	V
T	S	A	O	S	S	E	N	A	I
R	E	L	I	E	P	E	E	V	T
I	N	M	N	Q	H	C	R	I	R
T	A	O	X	L	A	M	V	C	O
N	H	U	U	S	B	L	O	O	P
E	M	R	O	I	R	E	S	A	S
R	A	R	T	A	S	T	O	L	E
B	E	L	E	G	A	N	T	E	D

Documento número 4

What type of person is this shop looking to employ?

Diálogo 2

Senhor Moura is being asked about the ages of his children.

Tania	**Senhor Moura, quantos anos tem o seu filho mais novo?**
Sr. Moura	**O mais novo, o Roberto, tem quinze anos.**
Tania	**E as suas filhas?**
Sr. Moura	**Pois, a Catarina tem dezassete anos e a Sonia vinte.**
Tania	**E o senhor? Quantos anos tem?**
Sr. Moura	**Eu? Ora bem, eu tenho . . . !**

quantos anos tem?	*how old is*	**anos**	*years*
	he/she?/how old are you?	**Ora bem**	*well now!*

Comentário

Talking about age, how old somebody is, in Portuguese is done in terms of saying how many years someone has. **Tenho X anos** is how you would say *I am X (years old)*. Having a birthday, is known as **Fazer anos: Quando faz anos?** *When is your birthday?* If you want to congratulate someone on their birthday, say **Parabéns!** *Congratulations!* If you are lucky enough to be invited to a family birthday (or other) celebration, be prepared for a wonderful feast!

Actividade

6 There are two sentences muddled up here. Can you unscramble them?

tem filha tem Quantos sua onze a anos Ela anos ?

Avaliação

You should now be able to do the following:

(*a*) Say this is my husband/wife.
(*b*) Say that is my brother/sister.
(*c*) Say this is our son/daughter.

(*d*) Say that is my youngest sister.
(*e*) Describe your husband/wife/teacher.
(*f*) Describe your own temperament.
(*g*) Ask someone how old they are.
(*h*) Say how old you are (you can be up to 20 at this stage!)

5
GOSTOS PESSOAIS
Personal tastes

In this unit you will learn

- how to say what you like/dislike
- how to say what you prefer
- how to ask other people about their preferences

Antes de começar

In this unit you will begin to find a mixture of forms of address. Remember that, between friends and young people, the **tu** form is used, and with older people, and people who do not know each other very well, you'll hear the polite forms of **o/a senhor/a**, or **o/a** plus the person's name. Don't forget that the verb will often be used on its own, without a real corresponding word for 'you'. When talking to more than one person, you can either use the plurals **os senhores/as senhoras** or simply the plural form of the appropriate verb. You will see this demonstrated in the first dialogue.

———————— Diálogo 1 ————————

Fátima is finding out if the Green family like Portuguese food.

Fátima **Então, os senhores gostam da comida portuguesa?**
Sr. Green **Gostamos muito. A comida é saudável e muito deliciosa.**
Fátima **Óptimo! A Senhora Green gosta de sardinhas?**

Sra. Green	**Gosto, mas não muito. Têm muito sal. Gosto mais de frango.**
Sr. Green	**Eu também gosto de frango. A nossa filha gosta muito de arroz de marisco.**
Fátima	**Não gostam do caldo verde? É tipicamente português.**
Sra. Green	**Gostamos um pouco. E a Fátima, gosta da comida portuguesa?**
Fátima	**Claro, sou portuguesa, e os portugueses gostam imenso de comida!**

os senhores gostam . . . . ? *do you (pl) like . . . ?*	**(o) sal** *salt*
a comida portuguesa *Portuguese food*	**gosto mais** *I like more*
	o frango *chicken*
gostamos *we (do) like*	**também** *also*
muito *a lot, very*	**o arroz de marisco** *sea-food rice*
saudável *healthy*	**não gostam . . . ?** *don't you like . . . ?*
delicioso/a *delicious*	**o caldo verde** *shredded kale soup*
gosta . . . ? *do you (he, she) like . . . ?*	**tipicamente** *typically*
as sardinhas *sardines*	**um pouco** *a bit, a little*
gosto *I (do) like*	**claro** *of course*
mas *but*	**gostam** *they like*
têm *they have*	**imenso** *a great deal, a lot*

Para estudar

1 More on -ar verbs

Gostar, like some of the verbs you learnt in units 2 and 3 (**morar**, **trabalhar**, **falar**) is what is known as a regular verb, i.e. it follows a normal pattern of endings for that group of verbs. It belongs to the biggest verb group in Portuguese – those which end in **-ar**. With only a few exceptions, all these verbs are formed in the same way:

● First you take off the **-ar** ending and you are left with what is called the stem.

> **Gostar** – ar = gost (the stem)

- Then you add on to this stem the appropriate ending according to whoever is doing the action.
- For **-ar** verbs, the endings you require are as follows:

stem +
– o	*I*
– as	*you* (informal)
– a	*he, she, you* (polite)
– amos	*we*
– am	*they, you* (plural)

Here are a few examples:

fal**o**	*I speak*	gost**amos**	*we like*
mor**as**	*you live*	mor**am**	*they, you live*
trabalh**a**	*he / she works / you work*		

The meanings are sometimes ambiguous, so to make sure you really know who is doing the action, you may need to use the words for *he* (**ele**), *she* (**ela**), or *they* (**eles, elas**).

2 *Gostar (de)* to like

The verb **gostar** is always followed by the word **de**, except when giving a straight like/don't like answer to a question.

Gosta **de** frango?	*Do you like chicken?*
Sim, gost**o**.	*Yes, I do (like it).*
Gosto **de** frango.	*I like chicken.*

The word **de** (which really serves no function in the sentence – it's one of those 'oddments' mentioned earlier in the book), combines with the words **o/a/os/as**, to form **do, da, dos, das**.

Gosto **do** frango.	*I like the chicken.*
Gostamos **das** sardinhas.	*We like the sardines.*
Ela não gosta **da** comida.	*She doesn't like the food.*

3 A lot, a little

You can describe just how much you do or do not like something by using words such as **muito** (*a lot, much*), **um pouco** (*a little bit*), **não muito** (*not much*), and **imenso** (*a great deal*). This last one is used a lot by Portuguese people.

———————— **Actividades** ————————

1 How would you say the following?

   (a) Do the senhores Brito like chicken?
   (b) Don't you (**tu**) like the shredded kale soup?
   (c) No, I don't (like).
   (d) We like sardines a lot.
   (e) Paula likes sea-food rice a little.
   (f) They like Portuguese food a great deal.

2 Choose the correct endings for the verbs in the sentences below. Here are the endings: **-o/-as/-a/-amos/-am**.

   (a) A Maria trabalh__ num hospital.
   (b) Eu (I) não gost__ do frango.
   (c) Nós (we) mor__ em Lisboa.
   (d) Tu não gost__ do caldo verde?
   (e) Os senhores Trindade fal__ inglês.

3 Match up the questions on the left to the most likely answers on the right. Remember some verb forms can refer to different people.

   (a) Tu gostas do arroz de marisco?   (i) Gostamos um pouco.
   (b) Os senhores gostam da comida?   (ii) O Miguel gosta muito.
   (c) A Paula não gosta do frango?   (iii) Sim, gosto muito.
   (d) Quem (who) gosta das sardinhas?   (iv) Não, não gosta.
   (e) O seu filho não gosta do   (v) Não, ela não gosta
       caldo verde?   muito.

Documento número 5

What would you choose to eat if you went to this restaurant?

Leitura

Listen to the passage and read it carefully. Nuno talks about his family's preferences for different countries. See if you can work out some of the reasons for their likes and dislikes.

Bom, gostamos todos da Suíça, porque é um país muito limpo, mas é um pouco caro para nós. Pessoalmente, prefiro a Austrália, porque tem um clima agradável. A minha mulher prefere a Dinamarca, porque ela gosta imenso da comida dinamarquesa. Não gostamos muito do Japão porque é muito movimentado. Preferimos um lugar mais calmo, como a Holanda. Os nossos filhos preferem o barulho. Eles gostam imenso dos Estados Unidos.

a Suíça *Switzerland*	**a Dinamarca** *Denmark*
porque *because*	**a comida dinamarquesa** *Danish food*
um país *a country*	
limpo *clean*	**o Japão** *Japan*
caro *expensive*	**movimentado** *busy, crowded*
para nós *for us*	**preferimos** *we prefer*
pessoalmente *personally*	**um lugar** *a place*
prefiro *I prefer*	**calmo** *calm*
um clima *climate*	**a Holanda** *Holland*
agradável *agreeable, enjoyable*	**preferem** *they/you prefer*
prefere *she/he prefers / you prefer*	**o barulho** *noise*

Actividade

4 Without looking back at the **Leitura**, see if you can answer these questions.

    (a) A família do Nuno gosta da Suíça?

    (b) Porquê? (*Why?*)

    (c) Porque é que o Nuno prefere a Austrália?

    (d) Eles gostam do Japão?

    (e) Quem prefere a Dinamarca?

    (f) Porque é que os filhos preferem os Estados Unidos?

Para estudar

4 Describing places

In unit 4 you learnt some words (that were adjectives) for describing people. In the reading passage you were introduced to some words to use when describing places (towns, countries), such as **limpo**, **caro**, and **movimentado**.

You might also want to try out the following:

barulhento/a	noisy	**barato/a**	cheap
sujo/a	dirty	**bonito/a**	nice, pretty (picturesque)
aborrecido/a	boring	**histórico/a**	historical
desagradável	unpleasant	**interessante**	interesting
moderno/a	modern	**cultural**	cultural
antigo/velho/a	old		

5 (O) que prefere? What do you prefer?

When asking people about their preferences about various items, you can ask them **(o) que prefere?**:

O que prefere – frango
ou sardinhas?

What do you prefer? Chicken or sardines?

You can also use **qual prefere?** (*Which do you prefer?*):

Qual prefere – o Japão
ou a Holanda?

Which do you prefer? Japan or Holland?

Don't forget to make the verb plural (**preferem**) if you are talking about more than one person.

Documento número 6

What kind of holidays is this advertisement inviting you to take this year?

 —————— **Actividades** ——————

5 Try out the following phrases using what you have just learnt.

(a) Say you prefer England because it's historical.
(b) Ask which Sr. Antunes prefers – Switzerland or Denmark.
(c) Say that Sonia prefers Italy because it's interesting.
(d) Ask which the senhores Oliveira prefer – America or Japan.
(e) Say that we prefer Holland because it's pretty.

6 Fill in the puzzle with words used to describe various places. The first word is put in for you.

Avaliação

Now see what you have learnt in this unit. Can you:

(*a*) ask someone (singular, polite) if they like children?
(*b*) say that you like sardines, a little?
(*c*) say that Miguel likes Portuguese food a great deal?
(*d*) ask Sr. Green if he doesn't like the shredded kale soup?
(*e*) say that you prefer Portugal because it's interesting?
(*f*) ask the senhores Oliveira which they prefer: Italy or Japan?
(*g*) say that we prefer Danish food?

6

EM CASA

At home

In this unit you will learn

- how to describe your house
- how to say where things are
- how to say there is/there are

Can you remember how *in* and *on*, and *in a* and *on a* are said in Portuguese? Have a quick look back at unit 3 to check that you are completely familiar with forms of these expressions before learning new ground in this unit.

Antes de começar

The word **casa** basically means *house* in Portuguese, although it encompasses the overall general idea of a residence. For example, you may hear Portuguese people speaking about their **casa**, when, in fact, they live in an apartment. In most cities in Portugal, you will find people living in some kind of apartment: some of them are ultra-modern, while others are very traditional flats in old buildings. In the smaller towns, and in the countryside, you will find more houses as we think of them. **Em casa** means *at home* and the expressions **vou a casa**, and **vou para casa**, both mean *I'm going* (vou) *home*.

Leitura

Roberto is talking about where he lives. Listen to the cassette and then read the passage. How much of it can you understand without looking at the vocabulary list?

> **Moro em Lisboa, num apartamento moderno. Fica no quinto andar dum prédio muito alto. O apartamento não é muito grande. Há dois quartos, uma sala, uma cozinha e uma casa de banho. Gosto muito do apartamento porque é fácil de limpar. O prédio tem elevador mas, de vez em quando não funciona. Esta é a única coisa de que não gosto!**

um prédio *building*	**é fácil de limpar** *it's easy to clean*
grande *big*	**(o) elevador** *lift*
há *there are*	**de vez em quando** *from time to*
o quarto *bedroom*	*time, sometimes*
uma sala *a living room, lounge*	**não funciona** *it doesn't work*
uma cozinha *a kitchen*	**a única coisa** *the only thing*
uma casa de banho *a bathroom*	**que** *that, which*

So, how did you get on? Did you manage to guess some of the names of rooms? Many Portuguese words are fairly similar to English ones, and if you stretch your imagination a little bit, you can often come up with the correct words. For example, **quarto** is similar to the English 'quarters' (as in 'living quarters'), **sala** is like 'salon' and **cozinha** like 'cuisine'.

Diálogo 1

Now listen to Ana Maria talking to a friend about her house in the country town of Elvas.

Ana Maria	**Gosto imenso da minha casa.**
Julia	**Como é a casa? É grande ou pequena?**
Ana Maria	**Bem, é bastante grande, e tem dois andares. Fica no Bairro da Boa Vista, e é típica da região.**
Julia	**Quantas assoalhadas tem?**
Ana Maria	**Em baixo há uma sala de estar, e uma sala de jantar, e também uma cozinha grande.**
Julia	**E em cima?**

Ana Maria **Em cima há dois quartos pequenos e um quarto grande com terraço e uma casa de banho bonita.**

Como é a casa? *What's the house like?*	**em baixo** *downstairs*
(o) Bairro da Boa Vista *Boa Vista borough, area*	**uma sala de estar** *living room*
típica da região *typical of the region*	**uma sala de jantar** *dining room*
quantas assoalhadas tem? *how many rooms are there?*	**em cima** *upstairs*
	com terraço *with a balcony*

Actividade

1 Look at the two house plans below. One of them is Roberto's apartment, and the other is the downstairs of Ana Maria's house. Which is which?

(a)

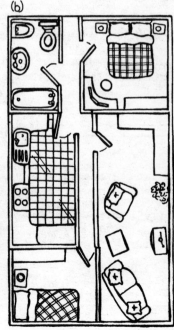

(b)

——————— **Para estudar** ———————

1 *Há* there is, there are

This small word is extremely versatile as you can use it to talk about both singular, or plural, objects:

Há uma sala.   *There is a lounge.*
Há dois quartos.   *There are two bedrooms.*

It can be used as a question: *is there, are there?*

Há uma cozinha?   *Is there a kitchen?*

and is turned into the negative *there is not, there are not*, by placing the word **não** before it:

Não há uma casa de banho.   *There isn't a bathroom.*

Comentário

In many Portuguese buildings, you will need to use the lift. It is vital then, to understand the symbols for the different floors. The ground floor is called **o rés-do-chão**, and in the lift you will see it abbreviated to **r/c**. All the other floors are simply numbered 1º, 2º, 3º, and so on. The º is the last letter of the appropriate number: primeir**o**, segund**o**, and so on.

——————— **Actividades** ———————

2 Look at the following house plan, and complete the dialogue below, to describe the house.

A casa da família Ferreira é antiga e ___ da região. Na casa há ___ quartos. Há dois ___ e um ___ com ___ . Em cima também ___ uma ___ ___ ___ . Em ___ há uma ___ uma sala ___ estar e uma ___ ___ ___ .

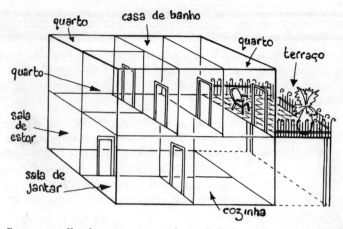

3   Can you talk about your own house? Start with **. . . a minha casa . . .**, and choose words from each box to help you with the description. If you need some help, there's a typical answer in the Key to the exercises.

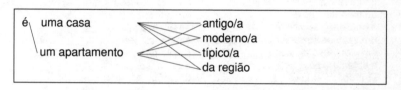

é   uma casa

um apartamento

antigo/a
moderno/a
típico/a
da região

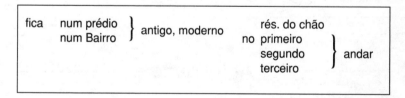

fica   num prédio   } antigo, moderno
       num Bairro

no   rés. do chão
     primeiro
     segundo   } andar
     terceiro

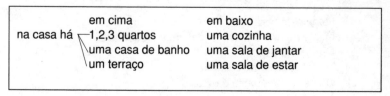

na casa há   em cima
             1,2,3 quartos
             uma casa de banho
             um terraço

em baixo
uma cozinha
uma sala de jantar
uma sala de estar

Gosto/não gosto da minha casa.

Leitura

Listen carefully to a 'through the keyhole' guide to Paula's house, as she describes where various pieces of furniture are located. Then read the passage below again, to make sure you have understood as much as you can.

Primeiro, estamos na sala, onde há um sofá em frente da lareira, e ao lado do sofá, duas poltronas. Há um vaso de flores em cima da estante. Na cozinha há um fogão entre o frigorífico e a máquina de lavar. O meu gato está debaixo da mesa. No meu quarto há um quadro bonito na parede, e detrás da porta há um armário. Na casa de banho há um chuveiro.

primeiro *first of all*	**a máquina de lavar** *washing machine*
onde *where*	
um sofá *a sofa*	**o gato** *cat*
em frente de *in front of*	**debaixo de** *underneath*
a lareira *fireplace*	**a mesa** *table*
ao lado de *next to*	**um quadro** *a picture*
a poltrona *armchair*	**na (= em + a)** *on*
um vaso de flores *a vase of flowers*	**a parede** *wall*
em cima do *on top of*	**detrás de** *behind*
a estante *bookcase*	**a porta** *door*
um fogão *an oven*	**um armário** *wardrobe, cupboard*
entre *in between*	**um chuveiro** *a shower*
o frigorífico *fridge*	

Actividade

4 Can you answer these questions, based on the passage?

   (a) Onde está o sofá?
   (b) O que há (*what is there*) em cima da estante?
   (c) Onde está o gato?
   (d) Há uma mesa na cozinha?
   (e) O que há no quarto da Paula?
   (f) Há uma poltrona na casa de banho?

——————— **Para estudar** ———————

2 In, on, under

The passage introduced you to some of the more common Portuguese expressions for describing where things (or people) are. These words are known as prepositions: the word *position* should help you to remember their function. Many of the Portuguese prepositions are made up of more than one word, and often end with the word **-de**. Did you notice in the passage how the de combined, or contracted, with the words for *the* or *a*? You should now be becoming familiar with these contracted forms – they are very common in Portuguese.

For example:

detrás d**a** poltrona (= de + a)   *behind the chair*
debaixo **duma** mesa (= de + uma)   *under a table*

You will meet more of these as you go along.

✳ Don't forget when describing the location of items which can move – use the verb **estar** for *is* (**está**) and *are* (**estão**).

 ——————— **Actividades** ———————

5 Look at the diagram of Jorge's **sala de estar**, and answer true (**verdadeiro**) or false (**falso**) to the following statements:

Na sala de estar:

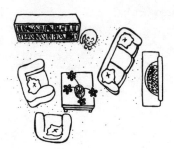

(a) Há três poltronas.
(b) O gato está detrás da estante.
(c) Há um vaso de flores debaixo da mesa.
(d) Há um sofá em frente da lareira.
(e) A estante está entre as poltronas.
(f) Há uma poltrona ao lado da mesa.

6 How would you say the following?

 (a) The cat is on top of the fridge.
 (b) There is a cupboard next to the bookcase.
 (c) Is there a sofa behind the table?
 (d) The shower is not in the kitchen.
 (e) The oven is next to the washing machine.
 (f) Is the cat in front of the armchair?

Documento número 7

 (a) How many bedrooms are there?
 (b) Is there a fireplace in the living room?

> # CASA DE CAMPO
> ## RIBATEJO
> Linda moradia, sala c/ lareira, 3 quartos, 2 wc, c/ quintal e garagem. Sossego e ar puro.
> Tel. 793 54 40/88 — Sr, Ferreira

Avaliação

You should now be able to do the following:

 (a) Say what kind of residence you have.
 (b) Describe which rooms your house has.
 (c) Ask someone what their house is like.
 (d) Say you have a big/small kitchen/bathroom.
 (e) Say that there are 2/3/4/5 bedrooms.
 (f) Say that there isn't a living room/dining room.
 (g) Say where your sofa is.
 (h) Describe where the fridge is.
 (i) Ask someone what there is in the bedroom.

7
A VIDA DIÁRIA
Daily life

In this unit you will learn

- how to talk about daily activities
- the days of the week
- the times of the day
- numbers 21–100

Antes de começar

In this unit you will be encountering the numbers from 21 to 100. You learnt from 0 to 20 in unit 3, so perhaps it would be a good idea if you revised them now before going any further. There's nothing worse than trying to learn a new set of words when previous ones are still rather vague. Listen to your cassette now, and you will hear ten numbers you have met before. Do you recognise them?

What about working the other way round? What would these numbers be in Portuguese?

12   6   18   2   15   10

If you are happy with these numbers, then on you go, if not, then spend a couple of minutes every day practising them until they are firmly planted in your mind – then you'll be ready for the next set.

Leitura

Rosa is describing her daily routine. Listen to and read the text, and see how many daily activities you can recognise. Also listen out for what time she does them.

Levanto-me às sete horas da manhã. Tomo banho e visto-me. Às sete e meia tomo o pequeno almoço, e saio para apanhar o autocarro às oito horas. Chego ao escritório às oito e vinte, e começo o trabalho às oito e meia. Ao meio-dia almoço. Saio do trabalho às cinco e um quarto e chego a casa às seis horas da tarde. Janto por volta das sete, e às quartas-feiras à noite vou a uma aula de inglês. Deito-me às dez menos um quarto.

So, how did you get on? The activities Rosa mentions are:

levanto-me *I get up*	**chego** *I arrive*
tomo banho *I have a bath*	**começo o trabalho** *I begin work*
visto-me *I get dressed*	**almoço** *I have lunch*
tomo o pequeno almoço *I have breakfast*	**janto** *I dine*
saio para apanhar o autocarro *I leave to catch the bus*	**vou a uma aula de inglês** *I go to an English class*
	deito-me *I go to bed*

The times of her activities mentioned were:

às sete horas da manhã *at seven in the morning*	**às seis horas da tarde** *at six in the evening*
às sete e meia *at half past seven*	**por volta das sete** *around seven*
às oito horas *at eight o'clock*	**às quartas-feiras à noite** *on Wednesday evenings*
às oito e vinte *at twenty past eight*	**às dez menos um quarto** *at quarter to ten*
às oito e meia *at half past eight*	
ao meio-dia *at noon, midday*	
às cinco e um quarto *at quarter past five*	

———————— **Para estudar** ————————

1 Two final types of verb

With the exception of **visto-me**, **saio**, and **vou**, all the verbs listed as Rosa's activities fall into the regular group of **-ar** verbs, the formation of which you learned in unit 5. Therefore, *she arrives* will be **chega**, *we begin* will be **começamos**, and *they dine* will be **jantam**. Have a quick look back at unit 5, if you cannot remember the various verb endings. **Visto-me** will be dealt with later in this unit, but the two remaining verbs belong to groups which follow different patterns for many of their endings.

Sair *to go out*			**Ir** *to go*		
I (eu)	saio	*I go out*	I (eu)	vou	*I go*
you (tu)	sais	*you go out*	you (tu)	vais	*you go*
he (ele)		*he/she/you*	he (ele)		*he/she/you*
she (ela)	sai	*go out*	she (ela)	vai	*go*
you (polite)			you (polite)		
we (nós)	saímos	*we go out*	we (nós)	vamos	*we go*
they (eles, elas)		*they/you*	they (eles, elas)		
you (pl)	saem	*go out*	you (pl)	vão	*they/you go*

2 *Visto-me* I get dressed

You will have noticed some of the verbs describing Rosa's activities had a **-me** joined on to them. Remember also, that you met this kind of verb in unit 1, when giving your name (**chamo-me**). The **-me** actually means '*myself*', and so the literal meanings of these verbs are – *I get myself up, I call myself, I get myself dressed*, and so on. When you want to talk about other people doing these actions, there are different 'self' words. Here is the verb *to get up* with all the appropriate end-words.

(eu)	levanto-me	*I get up*	(nós)	levantamo-nos	*we get up*
(tu)	levantas-te	*you get up*			
(ele, ela)	levanta-se	*he/she/you get up*	(eles, elas)	levantam-se	*they/you get up*

Be careful with the *we* form because it loses the final **-s** from the verb ending.

3 *As horas* time

The Portuguese talk about time in terms of hours (**as horas**)

A que horas ...?   *At what time ...?*

- Time on the hour is easily expressed as follows:

às	+	the number of	+	horas	+	{	da manhã
at		the hour		(o'clock)			da tarde
							da noite

às	sete	(horas)	da	manhã	7 a.m.
às	nove	(horas)	da	noite	9 p.m.

After the number, the **horas** is optional.

- Time past the hour is expressed thus:

às	+	the hour	+	e (*and*)	um quarto (*a quarter*)
					meia (*half*)
					... minutos (*minutes*)

às cinco e vinte	5.20
às três e um quarto	3.15
às oito e meia	8.30

Again, you may want to specify whether you mean morning, afternoon or evening.

- Time to the hour is expressed in a couple of ways. Here is one of them.

às	+	next full hour	+	menos	+	minutes/um quarto
				(*less*)		

às dez menos vinte	9.40

ao meio-dia	*at midday*
à meia-noite	*at midnight*
à uma hora	*at one o'clock*

4 Os números 21–100

To deal more effectively with time, you need numbers up to 60 at least, and as numbers are a part of our everyday lives, here is the next set for you to start learning.

21	vinte e um/uma	50	cinquenta
22	vinte e dois/duas	60	sessenta
23	vinte e três	70	setenta
24	vinte e quatro	80	oitenta
25	vinte e cinco	90	noventa
30	trinta	100	cem (cento)
31	trinta e um/uma	101	cento e um, *etc.*
40	quarenta		

Can you see the pattern of formation? You simply use the word **e** (*and*) to join the two lots of digits together. Don't forget, wherever one, or two occur, you must decide to use either the masculine or feminine form. There are two forms for 100: **cem** is used for a round one hundred, and **cento** for any combination over a hundred (101, 125, and so on).

Listen to the numbers on your cassette, and try to repeat each one in the pause.

 ———————— **Actividades** ————————

1 Look at Maurício's diary entry for Wednesday (**quarta-feira**), and complete the five statements about his daily activities.

Quarta-feira	
7.15 a.m.	levanto-me
8.30 a.m.	saio
9.00 a.m.	começo o trabalho
1.00 p.m.	almoço
5.20 p.m.	saio do trabalho
6.45 p.m.	janto
7.40 p.m.	aula de japonês
11.25 p.m.	deito-me

(a) O Maurício ___ às 7.15

(b) Começa o trabalho às ___ .

(c) Ele ___ às ___ menos ___
       ___ .

(d) Às 7.40 tem uma ___ ___
       ___ .

(e) O Maurício almoça ___ ___.

2 The numbers on the left represent the house numbers on the doors on the right. Can you match them up correctly?

(a) vinte e sete   (b) setenta e sete   (c) noventa e três
(d) trinta e cinco   (e) quarenta e um   (f) noventa e seis

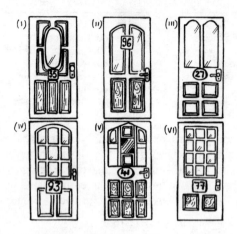

3 Match the clock times to the statements about the daily activities that various people do.

(i)   A Maria levanta-se às seis e meia.
(ii)   O Jorge almoça ao meio-dia e vinte.
(iii)   O Manuel sai do trabalho às cinco menos dez.
(iv)   A Lídia janta às sete e um quarto.
(v)   O Filipe chega ao trabalho ao meio-dia menos vinte.

4 Can you answer the following questions about your own daily routines? There are some sample answers for you to check in the Key to the exercises at the back of the book.

(a) What time do you get up?
(b) What time do you have lunch?
(c) What time do you arrive home?
(d) What time do you go to bed?

—————— Diálogo 1 ——————

Rui and João are talking about their weekend routines.

Rui   **A que horas se levanta aos sábados?**

João   **Geralmente às oito e meia. Eu e a minha mulher vamos às compras, e o nosso filho vai jogar futebol com os amigos..**

Rui   **E a que horas almoçam?**

João   **Em geral não comemos muito ao almoço. Jantamos por volta das sete horas. E o Rui?**

Rui   **Na minha casa também jantamos mais tarde, e depois saimos para passear na praça.**

João   **O que faz aos domingos?**

Rui   **Bem, a minha mulher levanta-se e come cedo, e parte para a igreja. Passamos o resto do dia em família, e não nos deitamos muito tarde.**

aos sábados *on Saturdays*	**para passear** *(in order) to stroll around*
geralmente/em geral *generally*	
às compras *shopping*	**a praça** *town square*
parte *departs*	**aos domingos** *on Sundays*
amigos *friends*	**come** *she eats*
vai jogar futebol *goes to play football*	**cedo** *early*
	a igreja *church*
comemos *we eat*	**passamos** *we spend*
mais tarde *later*	**o resto do dia** *the rest of the day*
depois *then, after*	**em família** *together, as a family*

—————————— **Para estudar** ——————————

1 *Os dias da semana* days of the week

segunda-feira	*Monday*	**sexta-feira**	*Friday*
terça-feira	*Tuesday*	**sábado**	*Saturday*
quarta-feira	*Wednesday*	**domingo**	*Sunday*
quinta-feira	*Thursday*		

The days of the week are 'numbered' – 2nd, 3rd, etc. They are all feminine words. The weekend days are masculine. In spoken Portuguese, it is usual to drop the word '**feira**', and speak in terms of **terça**, **quinta**, etc.

na segunda	*on Monday*
no domingo	*on Sunday*
às sextas-feiras	*on Fridays*
aos sábados	*on Saturdays*

2 *A que horas se levanta?* What time do you get up?

You may have noticed the changed position of the 'self' word, **se**, in this question. In Rosa's earlier description she said **levanto-me**. Whenever you have one of these verbs, known as reflexives, the reflexive bit of it (the 'self' word) is placed before the verb if a question is being asked.

3 *Não nos deitamos tarde* We don't go to bed late

This is another example where the reflexives change their position and go in front of the verb – wherever a negative is used. So you could have:

Levanta-se cedo.	*He gets up early.*
but	
Não se levanta tarde.	*He doesn't get up late.*

4 -*er* and -*ir* verb types

Up to now you have worked with **-ar** type verbs, and a few irregular verbs. There are two other main verb groups, examples of which you saw in the dialogue. They are **-er** and **-ir** groups.

comer *to eat*		**partir** *to depart/leave*	
eu	como	eu	parto
tu	comes	tu	partes
ele, ela, *you*	come	ele, ela, *you*	parte
nos	comemos	nós	partimos
eles, elas,		eles, elas,	
you (pl)	comem	*you* (pl)	partem

Can you see the similarities between the two? Earlier, you had the verb **visto-me** (*I get dressed*). This belongs to the **-ir** group (**vestir**), but the *I* person is slightly different.

5 *a, ao, à* to, to the

Like previous contracted forms, the preposition **a** (*to, at*) combines with the words for *the*, to form the following:

ao = a + o   aos = a + os   à = a + a   às = a + as

ao trabalho *to work*   à igreja *to (the) church*
aos escritórios *to the offices*   às casasto *the houses*

Documento número 8

When can you not visit this establishment?

Actividades

5 How would you say the following?

(a) I get up early.

(b) He does not go to bed late.

(c) What time do you (pl) get dressed?

(d) We do not get dressed quickly (**rapidamente**).

(e) What are they called?

(f) What time do you (informal) get up?

6 The following people have lost their verbs. Choose the correct form of the appropriate verb from the list underneath. The infinitive of the verb you want is in brackets at the start of each sentence.

(a) (**compreender**) Ele ___ (*understands*)

(b) (**partir**) A senhora ___ (*departs*)

(c) (**comer**) Nós ___ (*eat*)

(d) (**vivir**) Os senhores Neto ___ (*live*)

(e) (**subir**) Tu ___ (*go up*)

(f) (**beber**) O senhor Smith ___ (*drinks*)

parte	come	vivem	compreende
sobes	bebe	partes	vivemos
compreendo	comemos	subo	bebemos

Diálogo 2

Senhor Buisel has to get to the airport on time. He asks his neighbour what time it is.

Sr. Buisel **Bom dia Dona Ana Maria.**

Da. Ana Maria **Bom dia senhor Buisel.**

Sr. Buisel **Desculpe, mas a senhora sabe que horas são?**

Da. Ana Maria **São duas menos cinco.**

Sr. Buisel **Obrigado. Preciso de ir ao aeroporto. Até breve.**

> **Sabe que horas são?** *Do you know what time it is?*
> **preciso de** *I need*
>
> **o aeroporto** *airport*
> **até breve** *see you soon*

Para estudar

Que horas são? What time is it?

As with the time of day, earlier in this unit, asking and telling the time uses the word **horas**, and literally asks *what hours are they?* The answer follows the same form: **são . . .** (or **é**, with *one o'clock*, *mid-day* and *midnight*). All the other times *to* and *from* the hour are the same as those you learned earlier.

São cinco menos vinte.   *It's 20 to 5.*
É meia-noite e um quarto.   *It's quarter past midnight.*

Comentário

Senhor Buisel called his neighbour Dona Ana Maria. The word **Dona** is used as a sign of respect when talking to older ladies, whether they are married or not. You may also hear **a senhora Dona Ana Maria**. Both of these forms of address can be used with verbs to convey the polite form of *you.*

A Dona Patrícia está boa?   *Are you well (Dona Patrícia)?*

Portuguese forms of address are extremely varied, as you keep finding out. Remember to take your cues from the people around you, and, when in doubt, err on the over-polite side.

Avaliação

You should now be able to:

(a) Describe your daily routine.
(b) Ask someone what time they get up.
(c) Count to 100 out loud.

(d) Say that we do not go to bed until (**até**) 10.30 p.m.
(e) Ask Paulo what time he has lunch on Sundays.
(f) Say that you do not eat much on Tuesdays.
(g) Ask Jorge what time he goes to church.
(h) Ask someone what time it is.

8
O TEMPO LIVRE

Free time

In this unit you will learn

- what a Brazilian Portuguese speaker sounds like
- how to talk about activities you enjoy
- how to ask people what they like doing in their free time
- four very important verbs: *listen*, *read*, *see* and *do*

Antes de começar

Before tackling the new verbs you are going to meet in this unit, it might be a good idea to look back at the explanations about the basic verb types: unit 5 for **-ar** verbs and unit 7 for **-er** and **-ir** verbs.

 ———————— Diálogo 1 ————————

Some market research is being carried out in the street to find out what people like doing in their free time. Listen to the conversation and then read it over. The interviewer is talking to a group of three passers-by.

Entrevistadora	**Boa tarde. Com licença, posso fazer umas perguntas?**
Miguel	**Claro. O que quer saber?**
Entrevistadora	**O que é que vocês gostam de fazer no tempo livre?**

Miguel	**Ora bem. No meu tempo livre gosto de ouvir música clássica, e de pintar.**
José	**Eu gosto de ir à piscina, ou de vez em quando gosto de passear no campo.**
Entrevistadora	**E você? O que gosta de fazer no seu tempo de lazer?**
Ana	**Pois, gosto muito de ler, e de ver televisão.**
Entrevistadora	**E que gosta de ver?**
Ana	**Adoro as telenovelas brasileiras.**
Entrevistadora	**Óptimo!**

posso . . . ? *may I . . . ?*
fazer umas perguntas *to ask some questions*
claro *of course*
o que quer saber? *what do you want to know?*
o que é que vocês gostam de fazer? *what do you* (pl) *like to do?*
no tempo livre *in (your) free time*
no seu tempo de lazer *in (your) free time*
ora bem *well*

ouvir *to listen tc*
música clássica *classical music*
pintar *to paint*
a piscina *swimming-pool*
o campo *countryside*
e você? *and you?*
o que gosta de fazer *what do you like doing?*
ler *to read*
ver *to watch (see)*
a televisão *television*
as telenovelas brasileiras *Brazilian soap operas*

Para estudar

1 Você, vocês you

Did you notice that the interviewer spoke with a different accent? That's because she was Brazilian. She also used a different form of address than the ones you have already met. **Você,** and the plural **vocês**, is the most common way to say *you* in Brazil. The corresponding verb forms are the same as the singular and plural polite *you* in continental Portugal. The Portuguese tend to use the plural **vocês** also, but many prefer not to use the singular **você**, although you may hear it from time to time; this is the influence of the mighty Brazilian soap opera!

2 Posso? May/can I?

The usual reponse if someone asks **posso?** is **pode** (*you can*) or **sim pode** (*yes you can*) or even **claro que pode** (*of course you can*). Other forms of this verb you may need are:

tu podes
ele/ela pode
nós podemos
eles/elas/vocês podem

Posso? is what you would say if you wanted to take a spare chair from someone's table in a restaurant or café.

3 O que (é que) gosta de fazer? What do you like to do (doing)?

You should remember that in unit 5, the verb **gostar de** (*to like*) was used with various nouns (things) to describe what you do or don't like. Now you can use the same verb to talk about things you like doing, and as **gostar** is a straightforward **-ar** verb, you can also talk about other people's likes without too many problems.

O Nuno gosta de pintar.　　*Nuno likes painting (to paint).*
Gostamos de ouvir música.　　*We like listening to music.*

In addition to some of the activities listed in the dialogue, here are some more suggestions for things you may do in your free time.

praticar desportos　*playing sports*	**trabalhar no jardim/jardinar**
ir ao teatro　*going to the theatre*	*working in the garden*
nadar　*swimming*	**dançar**　*dancing*
andar　*walking*	**fazer bricolage**　*doing*
viajar　*travelling*	*'do-it-yourself'*
costurar　*sewing/making clothes*	**fazer colecção de**　*collecting . . .*

 ———————— **Actividades** ————————

1　See if you can do the following:

(a) Ask Maria what she likes doing in her free time.

(b) Say that you like sewing.

(c) Ask the da Silvas if they like travelling.

(d) Ask José and Nuno if they like playing sports.

(e) Say what you don't like doing.

(f) Ask someone you know very well if they like swimming in their free time.

2   You are walking through Oporto when you are stopped in the street by an interviewer who wants to find out what you and your family enjoy doing in your free time. As you are the only one who can speak Portuguese, you will have to speak for your family. Follow the prompts and complete the conversation.

Entrevistador	**Bom dia. Com licença, posso fazer umas perguntas?**
(a) You	*Say yes of course you can.*
Entrevistador	**São portugueses?**
(b) You	*No, you're not Portuguese. You're all English. Tell him which city you're from.*
Entrevistador	**Mas fala português?**
(c) You	*Say yes you speak some Portuguese.*
Entrevistador	**Muito bem. Então, o que é que gostam de fazer no tempo livre?**
(d) You	*Say that you like going to the theatre.*
Entrevistador	**E a sua família?**
(e) You	*Say that your husband/wife likes to work in the garden, and that your children like playing sports.*
Entrevistador	**E gostam de visitar Portugal?**
(f) You	*Say, of course!*

Documento número 9

Would you be interested in this establishment if you like artistic pursuits?

CENTRO DE LÍNGUA, ARTE E CULTURA

Monólogo 1

Listen to and read Sonia's account of the activities she enjoys doing, and how often she does them.

Gosto muito de ouvir música. As vezes ouço (a música) rock mas geralmente prefiro (a música) jazz. Aos fins de semana passo muito tempo a ler. Leio revistas e jornais, e gosto de livros românticos. Vou muitas vezes à biblioteca para ler.

às vezes *sometimes*	**leio** *I read*
ouço *I listen to*	**revistas e jornais** *magazines and newspapers*
aos fins de semana *at the weekend(s)*	**livros românticos** *romantic books*
passo tempo a ler *I spend time reading*	**muitas vezes** *often, many times*
	a biblioteca *library*

Monólogo 2

Now find out what Nuno gets up to, and when.

Gosto imenso de praticar desportos. Adoro jogar ténis, e todo os dias tento jogar pelo menos uma hora. Também faço colecção de selos, e todas as noites vejo a televisão. O meu programa preferido é Roda da Sorte.

jogar ténis *to play tennis*	**todas as noites** *every night*
todos os dias *each, every day*	**vejo** *I watch, see*
tento *I try*	**o meu programa preferido** *my favourite programme*
pelo menos *at least*	**Roda da Sorte** *Wheel of Fortune*
faço colecção de selos *I collect stamps*	

Para estudar

1 Sometimes, often, never

There are many words to describe how frequently people do activities; some appeared in the monologues (**às vezes**, **muitas vezes**, **todos os dias**, **todas as noites**), here are some further suggestions:

nunca *never*	**cada (mês)** *each (month)*
de vez em quando *sometimes*	**todos os dias** *every day*
uma vez por (semana) *once a (week)*	**poucas vezes** *few times, little*

In general, these expressions go before the verb,

> Nunca vou ao cinema. *I never go to the cinema.*

although some will fit naturally at the end of a sentence.

> Vejo a televisão todos os dias. *I watch television every day.*

2 Ouço, leio, vejo, faço I listen, read, see, do (make)

The verbs **ouvir**, **ler**, **ver**, and **fazer** are all irregular in some way or other. Here are the four verbs in full:

ouvir *to listen*			**ler** *to read*		
(eu)	ouço	*I listen*	(eu)	leio	*I read*
(tu)	ouves	*you listen*	(tu)	lês	*you read*
(ele, ela, você, o senhor)	ouve	*he/she listens/ you listen*	(ele, ela, você, o senhor)	lê	*he/she reads/ you read*
(nós)	ouvimos	*we listen*	(nós)	lemos	*we read*
(eles, elas, vocês, os senhores)	ouvem	*they/you listen*	(eles, elas, vocês, os senhores)	lêem	*they/you read*

ver	*to watch, see*	
(eu)	vejo	*I watch, see*
(tu)	vês	*you watch, see*
(ele, ela, você o senhor)	vê	*he/she you watch(es), see(s)*
(nós)	vemos	*we watch, see*
(eles, elas, vocês os senhores)	vêem	*they/you watch, see*

fazer	*to do*	
(eu)	faço	*I do*
(tu)	fazes	*you do*
(ele, ela, você o senhor)	faz	*he/she does/ you do*
(nós)	fazemos	*we do*
(eles, elas vocês os senhores)	fazem	*they/you do*

3 *Para* in order to

Sonia said she goes to the library **para ler** (*to read*), and you may have wondered why you needed the word **para**, when in fact **ler** means *to read*. This also arose in the last unit, when Rosa said she leaves her house **para apanhar o autocarro** *to catch the bus*. In fact you need to use the word **para** (*in order to*) before any verb, when it is your intention or objective to do something.

Vou à cidade para fazer as compras.

I go to town (in order) to do the shopping.

 ———————— **Actividades** ————————

3 Fill in the gaps in the monologue below, choosing from the words in the box.

Eu gosto de ler ___ de aventura. ___ todos os ___ , e também ___ a televisão. O meu marido ___ música clássica, e ___ golfe. Ele ___ ___ o jornal, mas ___ de ler revistas. As minhas filhas ___ à discoteca ___ as semanas, e de ___ em ___ ___ colecção de bonecas (*dolls*).

ouve	nunca	gosta	leio
vão	livros	joga	dias
lê	vejo	todas	vez
quando	fazem		

4 Link up the statements on the left, with the verbs on the right, using **para** (*in order to*) to make complete sentences.

(*a*)	Vou à biblioteca	(i)	fazer as compras.
(*b*)	Paula vai ao escritório	(ii)	dançar.
(*c*)	Vamos ao centro desportivo	(iii)	ler os livros.
(*d*)	Ela vai ao supermercado	(iv)	jogar tênis.
(*e*)	Eles vão à piscina	(v)	nadar.
(*f*)	Mónica vai à discoteca	(vi)	trabalhar.

5 Fill in the crossword puzzle with expressions of frequency. The first has been done for you.

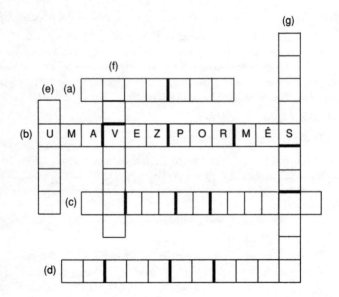

Documento número 10

How often is this restaurant open?

RESTAURANTE - BAR

2 IRMÃOS

ABERTO TODOS OS DIAS

Especialidades da Casa: CATAPLANA - BIFE À CASA - ENTRECOSTO
COZINHA TRADICIONAL PORTUGUESA - **ALMOÇOS** - **JANTARES**
_____ *AR CONDICIONADO*

SANTA EULÁLIA — TELEFONE: 54852 _____ 8200 ALBUFEIRA

Avaliação

Now see if you can do the following:

(a) Ask someone what they like to do in their free time.
(b) Say what you like doing.
(c) Respond to someone who has asked if they can take a chair from your table.
(d) Say what your husband/wife likes doing.
(e) Say how often you watch television.
(f) Ask Mr. and Mrs. da Costa if they often listen to music.
(g) Say you're going to town to go shopping.

9
AS FÉRIAS
The holidays

In this unit you will learn

- how to talk about holidays
- how to talk about where you will holiday this year / next year
- numbers 101 – 199
- months of the year
- how to talk about wanting to do things
- how to talk about events in the future

Leitura

Read the following passage from a travel brochure, and then answer the questions (1) to (5).

Onde é que vocês vão passar as férias este ano? Porque não passam tempo connosco na ilha do Paraíso? Temos tudo aqui para umas férias maravilhosas e relaxantes.

Podem andar nas praias douradas, nadar num mar azul-claro, ou passear no campo sossegado. Se gostam de praticar desportos, temos duas quadras de tenis, três piscinas, um campo de golfe, e desportos aquáticos. A ilha fica longe de todo o stress quotidiano, e oferece a oportunidade de se relaxar num ambiente natural e especial.

passar as férias *to spend (the) holidays*	**o campo sossegado** *peaceful countryside*
este ano *this year*	**quadra de ténis** *tennis court*
connosco *with us*	**um campo de golfe** *golf course*
a ilha do Paraíso *Paradise island*	**desportos aquáticos** *water sports*
tudo *everything*	**longe** *a long way*
maravilhoso *wonderful*	**quotidiano** *everyday*
relaxante *relaxing*	**oferece** *offers*
podem *you (pl.) can*	**a oportunidade** *opportunity*
as praias douradas *golden beaches*	**um ambiente natural e especial** *a natural, special atmosphere*
o mar azul-claro *clear-blue sea*	

1 Onde pode passar umas férias maravilhosas?
2 O que pode fazer nas praias?
3 Onde pode nadar na ilha?
4 O que há para fazer se gosta de desportos?
5 O que é que a ilha oferece?

———— Diálogo 1 ————

Fernando is talking to a colleague about where his family usually spends their holidays.

Fernando **Então, Júlio, vai tirar férias este ano?**

Júlio **Vou, sim. Vou para a Grécia. A minha mulher quer conhecer a cultura grega. E o Fernando? Onde vai?**

Fernando **Geralmente, viajamos pela Europa, e ficamos em vários países. Sempre gostamos de provar as comidas estrangeiras. E os seus filhos, Júlio? Vão com vocês?**

Júlio **Não. A minha filha nunca passa as férias connosco. Sempre vai com o namorado para a França. De vez em quando o nosso filho quer vir connosco, mas em geral prefere passar o verão na praia.**

tirar férias *to take / have a holiday*	**(o) país** *country*
a Grécia *Greece*	**sempre** *always*
quer *wants*	**provar** *to try, taste*
conhecer *to get to know*	**comidas estrangeiras** *foreign food*
a cultura grega *Greek culture*	**o/a namorado/a** *boy / girl friend*
viajamos pela Europa *we travel through Europe*	**a França** *France*
	vir *to come*
vários *various*	**o verão** *summer*

Para estudar

1 Two irregular verbs

A couple more irregular verbs you may want to use are **querer** (*to want*) and **vir** (*to come*). Here they are written out in the normal format:

querer *to want*	**vir** *to come*
quero	venho
queres	vens
quer	vem
queremos	vimos
querem	vêm

2 *Saber* and *conhecer* to know *or* to know

Both of the above verbs mean *to know*. **Saber** is used to mean to know a fact, or how to do something. You came across an example of it in unit 7. **Conhecer** means to know a person or place, and to get to know someone or somewhere. You would say

| Sabe que horas são? | *Do you know what time it is?* |
| Não sei. | *I don't know.* |

but

| Não conheço a Áustria. | *I don't know Austria.* |

Note: In the *I* (first) person, the c acquires a little tail (a cedilha) to maintain a soft-c sound.

3 *Pela Europa* through Europe

Pela is another example of those contracted word forms you keep coming across. It comes from the preposition **por** (*through, by*) + **o, a, os, as**, the full forms being **pelo, pela, pelos, pelas.**

| Pelo mar. | *Through the sea.* |
| Pelas ruas. | *Through the streets.* |

Actividades

1 Fill in your part of the dialogue, according to the instructions. You are discussing where you and your family spend your holidays.

Teresa **Onde passa as férias em geral?**
(a) You *Say you often go to Italy in the spring* (**na primavera**).
Teresa **Porque gosta da Itália?**
(b) You *Say you like Italian culture.*
Teresa **E os filhos também vão?**
(c) You *Say that your son always comes with you, but that your daughter prefers to travel with her boyfriend.*
Teresa **Onde quer ir nas férias de inverno** *(winter)*?
(d) You *Say that you usually stay at home, but that you and your family want to get to know France in the autumn* (**no outono**).

2 Choose the correct verb (**conhecer** or **saber**) to fill in the gaps in these sentences.

(a) Sabes que horas sâo? Não ___.
(b) A minha mãe ___ o tue irmão.
(c) A Paula e a Susana não ___ falar italiano.
(d) Vocês ___ o Brasil?
(e) Eu ___ nadar muito bem.
(f) Nós não ___ onde vamos passar as férias.

Diálogo 2

Daniela and Lúcia are discussing where they would like to spend their holidays, and where they are going to spend them.

Daniela **Lúcia, onde vais passar as férias este ano?**
Lúcia **Pois, em Março vou visitar a Inglaterra para passar tempo com a minha amiga inglesa. E tu, Daniela? Tens férias este ano?**

Daniela	**Tenho. Vou passar quinze dias na Espanha, em Novembro. A minha mãe diz que é muito bonita no outono. O que vais fazer para o ano?**
Lúcia	**Bom, o ano que vem gostaria de viajar pela Índia. E tu?**
Daniela	**Também gostaria de fazer uma viagem exótica, mas não tenho muito dinheiro. Provavelmente o ano que vem vou passar as férias na terra, em Braga.**

Março *March*	**gostaria de** *I would like (to)*
quinze dias *fifteen days* (= a fortnight)	**uma viagem exótica** *an exotic journey*
Novembro *November*	**o dinheiro** *money*
diz *says*	**provavelmente** *probably*
no outono *in the autumn*	**na terra** *in (one's) home town, region*
para o ano *next year*	
o ano que vem *next year*	

Comentário

The Portuguese are very attached to their home towns, especially those who come from country areas (**o campo**). Throughout history, the land (**a terra**), has played an important part in the lives of the Portuguese, as Portugal has been a predominantly agricultural country. It is not surprising, then, that the Portuguese refer to their home towns as **a terra**.

Nevertheless, they do like to travel, settling all over the world (at the last count more than four million Portuguese emigrants were scattered around the globe). But, despite their globetrotting, it is often to **a terra** that their feet turn when they feel **saudades** (a distinctly Portuguese feeling of the deep yearning for far-off places or people).

 ——————— **Para estudar** ———————

1 *Os meses do ano* the months of the year

Janeiro *January*		**Abril** *April*	
Fevereiro *February*		**Maio** *May*	
Março *March*		**Junho** *June*	

Julho	*July*	**Outubro**	*October*
Agosto	*August*	**Novembro**	*November*
Setembro	*September*	**Dezembro**	*December*

Note that the months in Portuguese do have capital letters, although you may find them written with small letters in Brazil.

2 Now or next year?

When you want to talk about things you do now, you use the simple parts of the verbs you have been learning – these are in the present time, i.e. what you are doing now, or what you usually do:

Sempre vou a uma aula
de francês.
I always go to a French class.

If you want to talk about an action which is going to take place at some point in the future, be it near or far in time, you can simply use the appropriate part of the verb **ir** (*to go*), plus the action verb.

Vamos visitar o Japão no ano
que vem.
*We're going to visit Japan
next year.*

Vou à cidade amanhã.
I'm going to town tomorrow.

3 *Gostaria de* I would like to

You know already how to talk about things you like, using **gostar de**. If you want to discuss something *you would like to do*, then you must use the form used by Lúcia in the dialogue: **gostaria de viajar** (*I would like to travel*). **Gostaria** is also the form for *he, she* and polite *you*. Add **-s** to it, and you have the form for *you* (**tu**) – **gostarias**. *We would like* is **gostaríamos**, and *they* (and *you* plural) is **gostariam**.

Actividades

3 Make six complete sentences using the components from the columns below. There is a variety of possible answers. Take care to match the correct verb form with the correct person form. You'll find some sample answers in the Key to the exercises in the back of the book.

(a)	Eu	vamos	trabalhar	pela Escócia	amanhã
(b)	Tu	vão	jogar	no mar	o ano que vem
(c)	Você	vou	tirar	no jardim	em Julho
(d)	Nós	vai	visitar	golfe	na sexta-feira
(e)	Os senhores	vão	nadar	férias	em Abril
(f)	Eles	vais	viajar	o meu amigo	no sábado

4 How would you say the following:

(a) I would like to visit Germany.

(b) Paulo would not like to work on Monday.

(c) Would you (pl) like to drink with us?

(d) My husband/wife would like to try Brazilian food.

(e) We would like to travel through America.

5 Can you find all the months hidden in this wordsearch?

A	J	U	L	H	O	B	F	C	O
D	D	E	I	F	G	H	E	I	R
S	E	J	R	K	L	O	V	M	B
E	Z	N	B	O	H	P	E	Q	U
T	E	J	A	N	E	I	R	O	T
E	M	R	U	S	T	O	E	U	U
M	B	J	V	W	X	Y	I	Z	O
B	R	A	B	C	O	Ç	R	A	M
R	O	R	B	M	E	V	O	N	M
O	T	S	O	G	A	D	E	F	G

Documento número 11

For which months is this train timetable valid?

COMBOIO DE FÉRIAS

PORTO-ALGARVE-PORTO

A partir de 30 de Junho até 10 de Setembro de 1995 realiza-se este serviço, com os horários e dias de circulação abaixo indicados:

20800/ /20801 ✕ Ⓡ 🚌 ① 1-2	20802/ /20803 ✕ Ⓡ 🚌 ② 1-2		ESTAÇÕES		20862/ /20863 ✕ Ⓡ 🚌 ③ 1-2	20864/ /20865 ✕ Ⓡ 🚌 ④ 1-2
6 30	20 45	P	Porto (Campanhã)	C	0 00	8 18
6 36	20 52		Vila Nova de Gaia		23 54	8 12
6 48	21 05		Espinho		23 41	7 58
7 15	21 33		Aveiro		23 12	7 27
7 47	22 10	C	Coimbra-B	P	22 38	6 53
7 48	22 12	P		C	22 36	6 52
8 52	23 16	C	Entroncamento	P	21 29	5 41
9 04	23 30	P		C	21 15	5 24
14 50	5 45	C	* Tunes *	P	15 18	22 47
14 54	5 53	P		C	15 08	22 41
15 03	6 03		Albufeira		15 02	22 35
15 18	6 20		Loulé		14 45	22 18
15 32	6 35	C	Faro	P	14 29	22 01
15 47	7 05	P		C	14 10	21 29
15 57	7 14		Olhão		14 01	21 20
16 20	7 43		Tavira		13 37	20 57
16 47	8 17		V. Real de S. António		13 10	20 26
16 50	8 20	C	V. R. de S. Ant.-Guad.	P	13 05	20 20

* Ligações de e para o Ramal de Lagos. Consulte os Cartazes Horários n.ºˢ ⑫ .

🔩 ————————— **Para estudar** —————————

Os números 101–199

If you really feel you know the numbers so far, then you'll be ready to go a bit further. You finished at 100 (**cem**, **cento**) last time. Here is the next group.

101	cento e um, uma	150	cento e cinquenta
102	cento e dois, duas	160	cento e sessenta
105	cento e cinco	170	cento e setenta
110	cento e dez	180	cento e oitenta
120	cento e vinte	190	cento e noventa
130	cento e trinta	199	cento e noventa e nove
140	cento e quarenta		

The pattern for the formation of these numbers is just the same as for the last group you learnt (see page 69).

cento e trinta e seis $100 + 30 + 6 = 136$

Don't forget, again, wherever 1, or 2, appear, you must decide on the masculine or feminine form. Portuguese currency is masculine (**o escudo**), but if you wanted to buy 122 beers, then you would have to ask for **cento e vinte e duas cervejas!**

 ——————— **Actividade** ———————

6 Say whether these sums are true (V = verdadeiro) or false (F = falso).

(a) Cento e cinco + trinta e um   = cento e trinta e seis
(b) Cento e noventa – vinte   = cento e quarenta
(c) Setenta e dois + quinze   = cento e vinte e dois
(d) Cento e sessenta – cinquenta   = cento e dez
(e) Cento e oitenta e três – oitenta e três = cem

Avaliação

See if you can now do the following:

(a) ask a group of friends where they're going to spend their holidays this year
(b) say that you want to get to know Greece
(c) say that your family always spends their holidays in Portugal
(d) ask someone if they know how to swim
(e) say where you are going to spend your holiday next year
(f) ask someone if they would like to come too
(g) say the months of the year out loud
(h) pick ten numbers at random between 100 and 199, and say them aloud.

10
TRANSPORTES
Transport

In this unit you will learn

- how to discuss travelling and travel arrangements
- how to talk about means of transport
- the numbers from 200 upwards
- how to give some orders!
- how to say more than and less than

Antes de começar

Before starting this unit, the last of the first part of this course, have a look back at unit 3, unit 7 and unit 9 to make sure you really know the numbers up to 199.

 ## Diálogo 1

Olivia and Luisa are discussing how they travel to work. Try to follow the dialogue first by listening to your cassette, and then by reading it a couple of times.

Olivia **Bom dia Luisa. Vais trabalhar hoje?**
Luisa **Vou, sim.**

Olivia **Queres uma boleia? Acho que vou passar à tua empresa.**
Luisa **Obrigadinha, mas não. Hoje vou primeiro ao dentista.
Vou de autocarro. Depois vou a pé para o trabalho.**
Olivia **Muito bem. Então, até logo.**

hoje *today*	**obrigadinha** *thanks very much*
uma boleia *a lift*	**o dentista** *dentist*
acho (que) *I think (that)*	**vou de autocarro** *I'm going by bus*
passar *to pass (by)*	**vou a pé** *I'm going on foot*
a empresa *company, workplace*	

Diálogo 2

Now listen to Senhor Pinto answering some questions about his travel to work.

Entrevistador **Senhor Pinto, como vai para o trabalho?**
Sr. Pinto **Bem. Geralmente vou de comboio. O meu trabalho fica fora da cidade, um pouco longe. Vou e volto todos os dias.**
Entrevistador **O senhor não tem carro?**
Sr. Pinto **Não tenho. Queria comprar, mas não tenho dinheiro, e o comboio é rápido e barato. Viajo mais de quinhentos quilómetros por semana.**
Entrevistador **E vai sempre de comboio?**
Sr. Pinto **Às vezes vou de camioneta, e se tenho uma reunião no Porto, vou de avião.**

como vai para o trabalho? *how do you get to work?*	**barato** *cheap*
	mais de *more than*
vou de comboio *I go by train*	**quinhentos quilómetros** *500 kilometres*
fora da cidade *outside the city*	
longe *far away*	**de camioneta** *by coach*
vou e volto *I go and return*	**se** *if*
o carro *car*	**uma reunião** *meeting*
queria comprar *I would like to buy*	**de avião** *by plane*
rápido *fast*	

Comentário

The Portuguese have a tendency to make many of their words appear smaller, more affectionate, or friendly. This is done by modifying the endings of words, usually adding **-inho**, or **-zinho**, among others. In the first dialogue, Luisa said **obrigadinha**, coming from the more usual **obrigada**. You will hear many people use this form of thanks. Other common words of this type you may come across may include: **coitadinho(a)**, from **coitado** (*poor thing*), **um livrinho**, from **livro** (*book*), and **pãozinho** (*bread roll*), from **pão**. Conversely, some words are made larger by the addition of **-ão**; so if you want a bottle of wine (**uma garrafa de vinho**), and you asked for a **garrafão**, you'd get a five-litre flagon!

Para estudar

1 De carro, a pé by car, on foot

Means of transport is, in the main, conveyed by **de**, plus the name of the vehicle. Thus you could travel:

de carro *by car*	**de barco** *by boat*
de comboio *by train*	**de bicicleta** *by bike*
de autocarro *by bus*	**de moto(cicleta)** *by motorbike*
de camioneta *by coach*	but **a pé** *on foot*
de avião *by plane, air*	**a cavalo** *on horseback*

2 Quero, queria I want, I would like

Queria is the polite form of the verb **querer** (*to wish, want*). You learnt this verb in the last unit. **Queria** is what you would use to ask for anything in a shop, ticket office, café, and so on. However, you also hear many Portuguese people using the usual form of the verb, especially on offering food or drinks, where in English you would probably use the polite form.

    Quer comer alguma coisa?   *Do you want to eat anything*
                                               (i.e. *would you like to?*)

3 *Mais de, menos de* more than, less than

In unit 4, you used **mais** (*more*) and **menos** (*less*) when talking about people being taller, shorter, older than each other. When discussing numbers – be it prices, distances, time – *more*, or *less than*, is expressed by **mais de** and **menos de**.

Mais de cinquenta libras.   *More than £50.00*
Menos de dez minutos.   *Less than ten minutes.*

4 *Os números 200 +*

If you are going to discuss distances, or be able to pay for things in Portugal, you will need to be confident with numbers into the thousands. Who knows, if you played the totoloto, you could end up winning hundreds and thousands of escudos – and who's going to count it if you can't? So, to help you on your way, here is the final group of numbers, from 200.

200	duzentos	**1,000**	mil
300	trezentos	**2,000**	dois mil
400	quatrocentos	**10,000**	dez mil
500	quinhentos	**100,000**	cem mil
600	seiscentos	**1,000,000**	um milhão
700	setecentos		
800	oitocentos		
900	novecentos		

You can help yourself to learn numbers by looking for pattern-groups.

5 cinco	15 quinze	50 cinquenta	500 quinhentos
8 oito	18 dezoito	80 oitenta	800 oitocentos.

The numbers in the 100s (200, 300, 400, and so on) also have a feminine form, to be used when talking about large numbers of feminine items. If you wanted to say 400 miles, you'd have to use **quatrocentas** with **milhas**.

The digits which make up the hundreds, tens, and units, are, in the main, divided in the same way as the last group you learnt – with the word **e** between each one. Hence, 953 would be: **novecentos e cinquenta e três**.

After thousands, there is usually no **e**. It only appears if the thousand is followed either by a numeral from 1-100, or by a numeral from 200–999 if the last two numbers are zeros.

1996 = **mil novecentos e noventa e seis**

Don't be daunted by numbers. Take every opportunity to practise them, and listen carefully when people tell you prices. When in doubt, you can always ask them to write things down. (**Pode escrever?**)

Actividades

1 Fill in the gaps in this monologue, choosing from the words listed.

Em ___ vou para o trabalho ___ autocarro. Vou e ___ todos os ___ . O autocarro é ___ e bastante (quite) ___ . Nos ___ de semana viajo ___ da cidade. ___ de comboio. Aos domingos ___ de passear de ___ . Quando vou de ___ , viajo de ___ ou de ___ .

volto	rápido	vou	férias
geral	dias	fins	gosto
avião	de	barato	fora
bicicleta	barco		

2 Listen to the list of numbers on your cassette, and see if you can repeat each one, and then write down what you think each number is.

Documento número 12

AUTOCARROS. Rua da República, 135. Tel. 23747/ 29624.

COMBOIOS. Tel. 22125.

TÁXI-AÉREO. Aeródromo de Évora. Tel. 28335.

Which of the telephone numbers would you ring for information about buses?

Leitura

Read this advertisement from a sales section of a newspaper, and try answering the questions following it.

Vende-se bicicleta

Quer melhorar a sua vida? Está farto de viajar no carro dos seus amigos, ou de pedir boleia aos seus pais? Tenho uma bicicleta bonita que você vai querer comprar. Com uma bicicleta, pode-se passear no campo, chegar mais rápido ao trabalho, e melhorar a saúde. Só custa quinze mil escudos. É barata! É bonita! É sua! Compre já!

1 O que é que a pessoa quer vender?

2 Como é?

3 O que se pode fazer com ela?

4 Quanto custa?

5 É barata, ou cara?

vende-se bicicleta *bicycle for sale*	**comprar** *to buy*
melhorar *to improve*	**pode-se** *one can, you can*
a vida *life*	**a saúde** *health*
estar farto de *to be sick of*	**só custa** *it only costs*
pedir boleia *to hitch a lift*	**compre já!** *buy now!*
os pais *parents*	

Para estudar

1 Vende-se, pode-se

Back in unit 7 you learnt some verbs, known as reflexives, where the word 'self' was included with the verb (*I wash myself*, and so on.). You will also find this kind of verb used in two more different situations. Firstly, when something is for sale, rent, on offer, and so on. Often the signs you see will say **vende-se** (*for sale*), **aluga-se** (*for rent*) or

oferece-se (*on offer*). In the bike advertisement (in the **Leitura**) what is actually being stated is that the bike 'sells itself', i.e. the actual vendor is not mentioned. You will also come across signs in shops or hotels which state **aqui fala-se inglês e francês**, (*English and French are spoken here*).

In the second example, **pode-se** means *one can* (i.e. you can – it is possible), again an unspecific, non-personalised form of the verb.

2 *De carro, no carro de X* by car, in X's car

Remember that transport is expressed by the word **de**. However, if you want to specify either someone's vehicle, or a timetabled train, bus, plane and so on you will use **em** (**no, na**).

no carro dos seus amigos	*in your friends' car*
no comboio das dez e meia	*on the 10.30 train*
no avião de TAP	*on the TAP plane*

3 *Compre!* Buy!

Ordering people to do things (however politely) can be rather confusing in Portuguese, so for the moment just have a brief look at the polite (you) form. With regular verbs look at what happens. Here are three examples:

Infinitive			Present tense		Polite command	
compr*ar*	*to buy*		compra	*he, she, you buy*	compre!	*buy!*
{ com*er*	*to eat*		come	*he, she, you eat*	coma!	*eat!*
{ part*ir*	*to leave*		parte	*he, she, you leave*	parta!	*leave!*

Have you noticed the pattern? The **-ar** verbs change to an **-e** ending, and the **-er** and **-ir** verbs change the other way, to an **-a**. To order more than one person, simply add an **-m** to the above forms (**comprem, comam, partam**).

Irregular verbs are awkward. Here are a few examples:

Infinitive		Singular	Plural	
fazer	*to make*	faça!	façam!	*Make!*
ser	*to be*	seja!	sejam!	*Be!*
estar	*to be*	esteja!	estejam!	*Be!*
ter	*to have*	tenha!	tenham!	*Have!*
ir	*to go*	vá!	vão!	*Go!*
vir	*to come*	venha!	venham!	*Come!*

You will pick up on other examples as you go along. In English these commands are usually followed by an extra word – more to give weight and rhythm to the command than for meaning. For example: *Have it! Go on/away! Come here!*

 —————— **Actividades** ——————

3 How would you say the following?

    (a) I go to work in my friend's car.
    (b) Paulo goes to the hospital by bus.
    (c) Ana is travelling on the 2.30 p.m. train.
    (d) Mr. and Mrs. da Costa are going on holiday by boat.
    (e) We are going to the cinema on the 7.15 p.m. bus.
    (f) Are you (**tu**) travelling by plane?

4 Select the correct command forms to complete these sentences.

    (a) (comprar – singular) ___ o carro!
    (b) (comer – plural) ___ as sardinhas!
    (c) (partir – plural) ___ hoje!
    (d) (viajar – singular) ___ de comboio!
    (e) (falar – plural) ___ menos rápido!
    (f) (beber – singular) ___ o café!

Avaliação

You have now completed the first ten units of the course, which have given you the basics of the Portuguese language. You have covered a lot of material, and before you go on to use your knowledge in the practical situations in the second part of the book, try this revision exercise to make sure you have all the information you need firmly established.

Can you:

    (a)   ask someone their name?
    (b)   say pleased to meet you?
    (c)   tell someone your nationality, and say where you are from?
    (d)   say that your husband/wife speaks Portuguese?
    (e)   ask a couple where they live?
    (f)   tell your friends where you work, and what your occupation is?
    (g)   say how old you are?
    (h)   describe someone in your family?
    (i)   ask someone if they like coffee?
    (j)   say that you prefer France?
    (k)   describe your house?
    (l)   say where your sofa/table/wardrobe is?
    (m) ask what the time is?
    (n)   describe your daily routine?
    (o)   ask a couple if they like to travel?
    (p)   say what you like doing in your free time?
    (q)   ask someone where they spend their holidays?
    (r)   say that you and you family would like to visit Spain?
    (s)   ask someone how they get to work?
    (t)   count to a million!?

So, how did you get on? If you managed to answer 15 or more confidently, then **Parabéns**! and on you go to unit 11. If you were unsure of any of these questions go over the units again, where you may have sticking points. Work through the exercises again, and use your cassette, until you are happy to move on.

11
VIAJAR
Travelling

In this unit you will learn

- how to talk about using public transport
- how to buy tickets
- how to get information at the tourist office
- how to ask for and understand directions

Antes de começar

Travelling on public transport in Portugal is an interesting option,
and it is generally cheap, efficient as well as a way of seeing more of
the country and its people. Once you have learnt a few basic phrases
for travelling, you will have a lot more confidence to get about.

 —————————— **Diálogos** ——————————

Read aloud the following short exchanges taking place at various
departure points for different means of transport.

Ao aeroporto at the airport

Senhor	**Faz favor, há autocarros para o centro da cidade?**
Informações	**Sim, há. O senhor sai do aeroporto e a paragem é ali em frente. Também pode tomar um táxi. A praça de táxis é lá fora.**

Ao porto at the port

Senhora	**Desculpe, a que horas parte o barco para Madeira?**
Senhor	**Às dez e quinze.**
Senhora	**E a que horas chega?**
Senhor	**Às quatro menos vinte da manhã.**

Na rua (1) in the street

Senhora	**Faz favor, há um estação de comboios aqui?**
Senhor	**Sim, a estação de caminho de ferro é ali, à esquerda.**

Na rua (2)

Senhor	**Onde é a paragem de autocarros para Lagos?**
Senhora	**É ali, à direita. Também pode apanhar um autocarro do terminal, que é ali atrás da praça.**

Num táxi in a taxi

Turista	**Para o hotel Vistamar se faz favor**
Taxista	**Muito bem.**
Turista	**Quanto é?**
Taxista	**São dois mil e quatrocentos escudos.**

o aeroporto *airport*	**a estação de comboios ferroviária**
a cidade *town/city*	*train station*
o centro *centre*	**a estação de caminho de ferro**
o senhor sai *you leave/go out*	**(C.F.)** *railway station*
a paragem *(bus) stop*	**à esquerda** *on/to the left*
ali/lá *there*	**o autocarro** *bus*
tomar *to take*	**à direita** *on/to the right*
um táxi *a taxi*	**apanhar** *to take (bus)*
a praça de táxis *taxi rank*	**o terminal** *bus terminus*
lá fora *out there*	**para** *to/for*
o porto *port*	**o hotel** *hotel*
parte *departs*	**quanto é?** *how much is it?*
o barco *boat*	**são . . . escudos** *it's . . . escudos*
chega *arrives*	

Actividade

1 How would you say the following?

(a) Are there buses to Lisbon (Lisboa)?
(b) The bus stop is over there on the left.
(c) The taxi rank is there on the right.
(d) What time does the train for Faro leave?
(e) At six fifteen in the evening.
(f) What time does the boat arrive?
(g) Is there an airport here?
(h) The bus terminus is over there, in front.
(i) To the port please.

Diálogo

Ana quer viajar de comboio. *Anne wants to travel by train.*

Ana	**Bom dia. Queria um bilhete para o Porto se faz favor.**
Senhor	**Quer de ida ou de ida e volta?**
Ana	**Ida e volta.**
Senhor	**Primeira ou segunda classe?**
Ana	**Segunda faz favor. É um rápido?**
Senhor	**Há um rápido-directo às duas horas.**
Ana	**Muito bem, então um bilhete para o rápido. Quanto é?**
Senhor	**Mil trezentos e oitenta.***
Ana	**Qual é a linha?**
Senhor	**É a linha número quatro.**
Ana	**Obrigada.**
Senhor	**De nada, bom dia.**

um bilhete	*ticket*	**muito bem**	*very well*
de ida/ida e volta	*single/return*	**qual?**	*which?*
um rápido (-directo)	*express*	**a linha**	*platform*
	(direct)	**de nada**	*don't mention it*

*The Portuguese colloquially refer to 1000 escudos as **um conto**; the ticket clerk above could have said, 'Um conto trezentos e oitenta'.

Comentário

Travelling by train in Portugal is extremely cheap and trains usually run on time. Apart from a few express trains running between the main cities, most trains are a similar type – rather like the huge silver trains of North America. There is a variety of tariffs, just as in the UK, depending on when you travel: most stations have information leaflets (**folhetos de informação**) with timetables (**horários**) and prices (**preços**).

You can also travel by coach (**camioneta**). The long distance coaches are very luxurious. You can usually only buy a single ticket, (**simples**) and you have to buy another single at the coach station (**rodoviária nacional**) on your return.

Actividade

2   Fill in your part of this dialogue, according to the instructions in italics.

Na estação C.F.

(a)   You   *Say good afternoon, I'd like two tickets to Loulé please.*
      Senhor   **Quer de ida ou de ida e volta?**

(b)   You   *Return please.*
      Senhor   **Primeira ou segunda classe?**

(c)   You   *First. How much is that?*
      Senhor   **São oitocentos escudos.**

(d)   You   *Which platform is it to Loulé?*
      Senhor   **É a linha número um.**

(e)   You   *What time does the train leave?*
      Senhor   **Às oito menos dez.**

(f)   You   *And what time does it arrive?*
      Senhor   **Às nove e vinte e cinco.**

(g)   You   *Thank you.*
      Senhor   **De nada. Boa tarde.**

Documento numéro 13

(a) Is this ticket a single or return?

(b) Is this ticket 1st or
2nd class?

 ——————— **Diálogo** ———————

Ao turismo at the tourist office

Turista	**Tem uma lista de hotéis da cidade?**
Senhora	**Aqui tem uma lista de hotéis, pensões e albergues. Também há um parque de campismo nos arredores da cidade.**
Turista	**E tem uma planta da cidade?**
Senhora	**Temos esta, e um mapa da região.**
Turista	**E tem informações sobre a cidade, as lojas, as atracções..?**
Senhora	**Aqui tem.**

tem . . . ? *do you have?*	**nos arredores** *on the outskirts*
uma lista *a list*	**uma planta** *town plan*
hotéis (um hotel) *hotels (hotel)*	**um mapa** *map*
pensões (uma pensão) *guest houses (house)*	**a região** *region*
albergues *hostels*	**informações** *information*
um parque de campismo *camp site*	**as lojas** *shops*
	as atracções *attractions*

Leitura

Read the following extract from a tourist information leaflet, and see how much you can understand.

Albufeira
Típica cidade de pescadores. Ambiente jovem. Praias entre roche-dos e falésias de cor vermelha.

Armação de Pêra
Areal extenso. Próximo pequenas praias tranquilas. Centro turístico.

Gastronomia
Deliciosos pratos de peixe e maris-cos. Destaque especial para as suculentas cataplanas e as sardi-nhas assadas. Doces de amêndoa e figo. A cozinha internacional de qualidade.

Quinta do Lago
Complexo turístico. Lago artificial. Extenso areal. Campo de golfe.

Silves
Capital do Algarve durante a ocu-pação árabe e até ao século XVI. Interessante castelo e catedral gótica.

Vinho
O solo algarvio, aquecido pelo sol, produz vinhos brancos e tintos ave-ludados. O vinho de Lagoa já ganhou renome mundial.

típico(a) *typical*	**doces de amêndoa e figo** *almond and fig sweets*
pescadores *fishermen*	
ambiente *atmosphere*	**a cozinha** *cuisine*
jovem *young*	**lago artificial** *artificial lake*
rochedos e falésias de cor vermelha *red cliffs and crags*	**campo de golfe** *golf course*
	durante *during*
areal extenso *long stretch of sandy beach*	**a ocupação árabe** *the Arab occupation*
próximo *nearby*	**o século** *century*
tranquilas *calm*	**catedral gótica** *gothic cathedral*
deliciosos pratos *delicious dishes*	**o solo algarvio** *the Algarve ground*
destaque especial para *special emphasis on*	**aquecido pelo sol** *warmed by the sun*
suculentas *tasty*	**produz** *produces*
cataplanas *cataplana-cooked dishes*	**aveludados** *velvet-like*
	já ganhou renome mundial *has already won world acclaim*
sardinhas assadas *grilled sardines*	

 ## Actividade

3 Can you answer these questions on the information contained in the **folheto**?

(a) Armação de Pera é bom para os turistas?

(b) O que há em Silves?

(c) Qual é a comida típica do Algarve?

(d) Onde se pode jogar golfe?

(e) O Algarve produz vinho verde?

(f) Que tipo de cidade é Albufeira?

 ## Diálogos

Read and listen to the following dialogues and at the same time look at the town centre map.

À *porta do turismo* outside the tourist office

Senhor **Faz favor, onde fica a estação de caminho de ferro?**

Transeunte **O senhor vira aqui à esquerda, toma a segunda rua à direita, segue sempre em frente, e a estação fica a esquerda.**

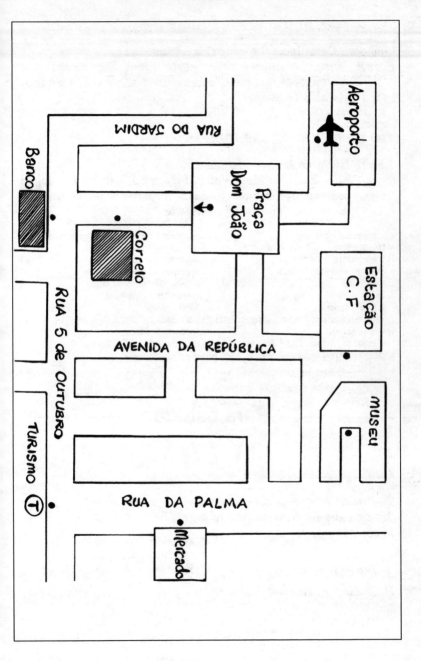

Na praça in the town square

Senhora **Desculpe, sabe onde fica o banco?**

Senhor **Sim. O banco é muito perto daqui. Siga sempre em frente até o correio, depois vire à esquerda, e o banco é ali à esquina.**

No mercado at the market

Isabel **Nuno, tu sabes onde fica o museu?**

Nuno **Sim. É muito fácil. Vai lá fora, vira à direita, e segue sempre em frente. Toma a terceira à esquerda e o museu fica mesmo ali em frente.**

(onde) fica *(where) is situated*	**até** *until/up to*
transeunte *passer-by*	**o correio** *post office*
là fora *(there) outside*	**à esquina** *on the corner*
vira, vire *turn*	**sabe, sabes** *you know*
toma *take*	**o museu** *museum*
a rua *road*	**fácil** *easy*
segue, siga em frente *carry straight on*	**vai** *go*
	terceira *third*
o banco *bank*	**mesmo ali** *right there*
perto (daqui) *near (here)*	

Para estudar

Giving directions

The main verbs used in directing people are: **tomar** (*to take*), **virar** (*to turn*), **seguir** (*to follow*) and **ir** (*to go*).

Toma a segunda rua.   *You take* (familiar) *the second road.*

Vire aqui à esquerda.   *You turn* (polite) *right there.*

Depending on how well you know the person the verb-endings may well differ.

	Very polite	Polite (Você)	Familiar (Tu)
o senhor a senhora }	toma vira segue vai	tome vire siga vá	toma vira segue vai

The last two columns are known as commands.

Actividade

4 Look at the map again on page 111 and see if you could give directions (in the polite form) to the following places (in each case imagine you are standing outside the starting point with your back to it).

(a) from the **turismo** to the **banco**
(b) from the **correio** to the **mercado**
(c) from the **museu** to the **estação**
(d) from the **aeroporto** to the **Turismo**

5 Now follow these directions and see if you can discover where you have been sent.

(a) Start at the **museu**: Siga em frente e vire à direita. Depois vá em frente e o ___ fica à esquerda.

(b) Start at the **banco**: Vá lá fora e vire à direita. Tome a primeira à esquerda e siga sempre em frente, até a ___ que fica à esquerda.

(c) Start at the **estação**: Vire à direita e vá sempre em frente. Tome a segunda à esquerda. Depois siga sempre em frente e o ___ fica à direita.

12

NA CIDADE

In town

In this unit you will learn

- how to exchange money
- how to buy stamps and make phone calls
- how to recognise a few public signs
- how to find a loo in Portugal!

You are going to come across a lot of numbers in this unit. This will be excellent practice. However, you might want to revise the numbers in units 3, 7, 9 and 10.

Diálogo

No banco in the bank

Senhora	**Bom dia. Posso trocar cheques de viagem por favor?**
Senhor	**Claro. Quanto quer trocar?**
Senhora	**Tenho cinco cheques de vinte libras cada.**
Senhor	**Portanto, cem libras esterlinas. Tem documentos – passaporte?**
Senhora	**Aqui está.**
Senhor	**E qual é a sua morada aqui em Portugal?**
Senhora	**É o Hotel Dom Luís, Rua 5 de Outubro, Albufeira.**
Senhor	**Faz favor de assinar os cheques. Obrigado. Agora, quer ir à caixa?**

trocar *to change*	**cada** *each*
cheques de viagem *traveller's*	**portanto** *so*
cheques	**o passaporte** *passport*
por favor *please*	**a morada** *address*
claro *of course*	**faz favor de . . .** *please . . .*
quanto . . . ? *how much . . . ?*	**assinar** *to sign*
libras (esterlinas) *pounds*	**ir** *to go*
(sterling)	**à caixa** *at, to the cash desk*

Comentário

You won't have any problems finding a bank in Portugal. Many of the larger towns and tourist areas have modern banks, with services such as the **multibanco** machines. Inside the bank look for the exchange sign (**câmbio**) on the counter. Sometimes you are handed a small disc with a number on it, known as **uma chapa**. You need to take this to the **caixa** and wait for your number to be called, they will then deal with your cash.

Díalogo

No correio at the post office

Sandra	**Olá, queria oito selos para Inglaterra, e dois para Alemanha se faz favor.**
Senhora	**São para cartas, ou postais?**
Sandra	**Três cartas e sete postais.**
Senhora	**Bom, são oitocentos e cinquenta escudos ao todo.**
Sandra	**Queria fazer uma chamada também.**
Senhora	**Quer passar para a cabine um.**
Sandra	**Obrigada.**

um selo *stamp*	**fazer uma chamada** *to make a*
para cartas/postais *for letters /*	*phone call*
postcards	**passar** *to pass*
ao todo *in total, all*	**a cabine** *booth*

———————— **Actividade** ————————

1 Match up the questions with the replies underneath.

(i) Qual é a sua morada aqui em Portugal?
(ii) Para cartas, ou postais?
(iii) Quanto quer trocar?
(iv) Possar trocar cheques de viagem?
(v) Tem passaporte?

(a) Tenho três cheques de dez libras.
(b) É o apartamento Sol, Praça São João, Loulé.
(c) Claro. Quanto quer trocar?
(d) Para cinco cartas.
(e) Aqui está.

Comentário

Making phone calls from Portugal is very expensive. Calls from your hotel, or from the post office, are always at an inflated rate. If you have to call home, find a telephone box (**uma cabine telefónica**) – some are now operated by telephone cards (**um cartão de chamadas**) available at post offices.

Public signs and notices

Can you guess what any of the following signs mean in English? (Answers in the key at the back of the book on page 185)

(a) PARA CRIANÇAS	(e) PERIGO
(b) NÃO FUMAR	(f) SAIDA DE EMERGÊNCIA
(c) PROIBIDO ESTACIONAR	(g) ENTRADA PROIBIDA
(d) ABERTO DAS 10.00 ÀS 12.00	(j) FECHADO

Proibido Estacionar
entre as 13:00 e as
15:00 horas.

Saida de Emergência
Lojas Primavera.

Documento número 14

Look at the following sign and answer the questions on it.

(*a*) What can you not do here?
(*b*) Why?

Loos!

Public conveniences are difficult to find in Portugal. It is common practice to use the toilet in a bar, café or even hotel. There are various names for toilets:

a casa de banho *bathroom*	**a privada** *the actual loo*
os serviços *public loos*	**os lavabos** *washroom and toilet*
a retrete *separate toilet*	

———— Actividade ————

2 Find the missing words from each phrase below, and fit them onto the crossword grid.

(*a*) Duzentas libras ___ .
(*b*) Tem ___ ?
(*c*) Qual é a sua ___ em Portugal?
(*d*) Sete ___ para Espanha por favor.
(*e*) Posso ___ cheques de viagem?
(*f*) Quer ___ os cheques?

(g) Para ___ ou postais?
(h) Quer esperar à ___ ?

13

IR ÀS COMPRAS

Going shopping

In this unit you will learn

- how to buy produce at a market
- how to deal with shops
- how to get by in shopping centres.

Antes de começar

Shopping in Portugal can be a great learning experience, and lots of fun, especially if you look for fresh produce at the market (**o mercado**), or if you try haggling for a bargain (**uma pechincha**) at the weekly, or monthly market (**a feira**). Larger cities now have supermarket chains (**os supermercados**), as well as shopping centres (**os centros comerciais**), hypermarkets (**hipermercados**), and all towns have at least a few **minimercados**. However, to practise the language, you need to venture into the smaller shops (**as lojas**), where you will have direct contact with the Portuguese people. So, **vamos às compras!**

Diálogo

No mercado at the market

Listen to the dialogue and then read it in the book.

Senhora Silva	**Bom dia, minha senhora. Tem laranjas hoje?**
Vendedora	**Tenho, sim. Quantas quer?**
Senhora Silva	**Dê-me dois quilos se faz favor. A quanto é o repolho hoje?**
Vendedora	**A cento e cinquenta cada.**
Senhora Silva	**Então levo dois. E há cenouras?**
Vendora	**Há, sim.**
Senhora Silva	**Bom, pois quero meio quilo.**
Vendedora	**Que mais?**
Senhora Silva	**Também queria umas peras. Estão boas hoje?**
Vendedora	**Estão boas mas um pouco maduras.**
Senhora Silva	**Ah, maduras não quero. Está bem, então é tudo.**

laranjas *oranges*		**levo** *I'll take*	
hoje *today*		**cenouras** *carrots*	
quantas? *how many?*		**meio quilo** *½ kilo*	
dê-me *give me*		**que mais?** *what else?*	
quilos *kilos*		**peras** *pears*	
a quanto é . . . ? *what price is the . . . ?*		**maduras** *ripe*	
o repolho *cabbage*		**é tudo** *that's all*	

 —————— **Para estudar** ——————

If you are buying produce at the market, you may need some of the following vocabulary.

Legumes *vegetables*	**Frutas** *fruit*
(as) cenouras *carrots*	**(as) maçãs** *apples*
(as) batatas *potatoes*	**(as) laranjas** *oranges*
(o) repolho *cabbage*	**(as) peras** *pears*
(a) couve-flor *cauliflower*	**(os) morangos** *strawberries*
(o) alho-porro *leek*	**(as) bananas** *bananas*
(o) pimentão *green pepper*	**(o) limão** *lemon*
(os) tomates *tomatoes*	**(o) melão** *melon*
(as) cebolas *onions*	**(a) melancia** *water-melon*
(os) cogumelos *mushrooms*	**(o) ananás** *pineapple*
(o) alface *lettuce*	**(as) ameixas** *plums*

Peixe *fish*	**Carne** *meat*
(o) atum *tuna*	**carne de porco** *pork*
(a) sardinha *sardine*	**carne de vaca** *beef*
(o) carapau *mackerel*	**(o) perú** *turkey*
(o) bacalhau *salted cod*	**(o) frango** *chicken*
(o) peixe-espada *scabbard*	**carne de vitela** *veal*
(o) espadarte *swordfish*	**(o) cabrito** *kid*
(a) pescada *hake*	**(o) javalí** *wild-boar*
(o) linguado *sole*	**(o) leitão** *suckling pig*
(os) mariscos *seafood*	**(o) fígado** *liver*
(as) lulas *squid*	**(as) tripas** *tripe*

When buying meat, you might need the names of the different cuts :

(a) costeleta *chop*	**um quarto** *a joint*
(o) escalope *scallop (thick sliced)*	**uma asa** *a wing*
(o) entrecosto *entrecôte*	**uma coxa** *chicken drumstick/thigh*
(a) fatia *slice (thin)*	

And don't forget your weights (in metric of course!)

um quilo de *a kilo of*	**250 gramas de** *250 g of*
meio quilo de *half a kilo of*	**100 gramas de** *100 g of*

Wordsearch

Can you find the names of ten items of fresh produce on this grid?

M	E	L	A	N	C	I	A	A	B
C	U	A	P	A	R	A	C	D	E
F	G	E	I	H	I	J	K	S	L
M	R	N	M	M	P	Q	A	R	J
A	S	R	E	P	O	L	H	O	A
N	T	U	N	V	U	W	X	Y	V
A	Z	A	T	L	B	C	D	E	A
N	F	G	A	J	N	A	R	A	L
A	H	I	O	J	K	L	M	N	I
B	E	S	P	A	D	A	R	T	E

Diálogo

Na mercearia in the grocer's shop

Freguesa	**Boa tarde senhor Maurício, como está?**
Senhor Maurício	**Bem, obrigado. E a senhora?**
Freguesa	**Estou bem. Olhe, preciso de comprar algumas coisas.**
Senhor Maurício	**Então, diga lá.**
Freguesa	**Quero meia dúzia de ovos, um litro de leite magro, um pacote de manteiga e uma garrafa de azeite.**
Senhor Maurício	**O azeite só temos desta qualidade; o mais barato acabou-se ontem.**
Freguesa	**Não faz mal. Levo este. Tem fiambre?**
Senhor Maurício	**Temos este, que é muito bom, e também temos este presunto aqui.**
Freguesa	**Pode cortar-me cinco fatias deste presunto aqui? E quanto é aquele queijo lá ao fundo?**
Senhor Maurício	**Aquele queijo da Serra custa mil e duzentos o quilo.**
Freguesa	**Então, dê-me trezentos gramas por favor.**
Senhor Maurício	**Mais alguma coisa?**
Freguesa	**É só. Obrigada. Quanto é?**
Senhor Maurício	**Ora bem, são quatro mil, duzentos e quarenta e dois ao todo.**

freguesa	*customer*	**azeite**	*olive oil*
olhe	*look*	**qualidade**	*quality*
preciso de	*I need to*	**o mais barato**	*the cheaper (one)*
comprar	*to buy*	**acabou-se**	*ran out (finished)*
algumas coisas	*some things*	**ontem**	*yesterday*
diga lá	*tell (me) then*	**não faz mal**	*don't worry*
meia dúzia	*half a dozen*	**fiambre**	*boiled ham*
ovos	*eggs*	**presunto**	*smoked ham*
um litro	*litre*	**queijo (da Serra)**	*(Serra) cheese*
leite (magro)	*(skimmed) milk*	**ao fundo**	*at the back*
um pacote	*packet*	**custa**	*costs*
manteiga	*butter*	**mais alguma coisa?**	*anything else?*
uma garrafa	*bottle*		

Para estudar

Here are some more everyday items you may need at the grocers:

(o) pão (de forma) *bread (sliced)*	**(a) água** *water*
(a) geléia *jam*	**(o) bolo** *cake*
(as) bolachas *biscuits*	**(a) sopa** *soup*
(as) ervilhas *peas*	**(o) sabão** *soap*
(os) fósforos *matches*	**(o) papel higiénico** *toilet paper*
(a) pasta de dentes *toothpaste*	
(o) mel *honey*	

You will also need the following vocabulary:

uma caixa de *a box (of)*	**um frasco** *a jar*
uma garrafa *bottle*	**um garrafão** *demi-john*
uma lata *tin, can*	**uma barra** *bar*
um pacote *packet*	**um tubo** *tube*
um rolo *roll*	

Actividade

1 Alice has got her shopping list in a muddle, so her items and quantities are jumbled. Can you match the two items correctly?

um quilo de	presunto
3 costeletas de	água
6 fatias de	cenouras
um pacote de	bolachas
2 latas de	pasta de dentes
uma garrafa de	porco
um tubo de	sopa
uma dúzia de	ovos

Documento número 15

Mandy wanted to buy some tuna. Did she get any?

```
SUPERMERCADO  SILVA
LARGO DE SANTA MARIA, 26
7645 VILA NOVA MILFONTES
   CONT.N.801661528



  C   1      SCONTR  367

 AGUA CRUZE 17%        75.00
 ATUM CALVO 17%       110.00
     2    X    80.00
 IOG.PEDAC. 17%       160.00
 PLANTA 250 17%       132.50
 **TOTAL**          477.50
 NUMERARIO           5000.00
 TROCO              4522.50

 CAIXA 3    UNID       5
        O B R I G A D O

 07-08-1995  17:05
```

Leitura

Listen to this passage all about buying clothes and then read it carefully in the book. Use the word box at the end only if you really get stuck.

Em Portugal há vários lugares onde se pode comprar roupa; da feira ao centro comercial e às casas de modas. As roupas e os sapatos portugueses são muito elegantes. Na Casa de Modas Silvana podem-se comprar roupas para homens (calças, camisas, gravatas, jaquetas) e para mulheres (vestidos, blusas, saias, conjuntos), como também os bonitos sapatos, sandálias e botas que estão na moda. Há roupas em vários estilos, cores e tamanhos. A senhora Ferreira quer comprar uma blusa. Ela procura um padrão de que gosta e pergunta se pode experimentar. Quando sai da cabine de provas pergunta se há a mesma blusa num tamanho maior, e em verde. Ela não gosta muito da azul. Há muitas cores –

vermelho, amarelo, rosa, branco, preto e laranja, além de azul-claro e verde-escuro. A senhora Ferreira escolhe uma blusa em preto, depois experimenta um par de sapatos de salto alto, de cabedal. Ela calça o número 44, e os sapatos servem-lhe perfeitamente.

vários lugares *various places*	**a cabine de provas** *changing room*
da . . . ao *. . . from the . . . to the . . .*	**pergunta** *she asks*
a casa de modas *fashion house*	**a mesma blusa** *the same blouse*
os sapatos *shoes*	**maior** *bigger*
elegantes *elegant*	**em verde** *in green*
roupas para . . . *clothes for*	**azul** *blue*
homens / mulheres *men / women*	**vermelho** *red*
calças *trousers*	**amarelo** *yellow*
camisas *shirts*	**rosa** *pink*
gravatas *ties*	**branco** *white*
jaquetas *jackets*	**preto** *black*
vestidos *dresses*	**laranja** *orange*
blusas *blouses*	**além de** *as well as*
saias *skirts*	**azul-claro** *light blue*
como também *as well as*	**verde-escuro** *dark green*
sandálias *sandals*	**escolhe** *she chooses*
botas *boots*	**experimenta** *she tries*
na moda *in fashion*	**um par** *a pair*
estilos, padrão *styles, style*	**de salto alto** *high-heeled*
cores *colours*	**de cabedal** *in leather*
tamanhos *sizes*	**calça** *she takes (shoes)*
para si *for herself*	**o número 44** *size 44*
procura *she is looking for*	**servem-lhe perfeitamente** *fit her perfectly*
experimentar *to try on*	**conjuntos** *suits*
sai *she leaves*	

Actividades

2 Can you answer these questions based on the text?

- (a) Onde se podem comprar roupas em Portugal?
- (b) Os sapatos portugueses são elegantes?
- (c) Podem-se comprar roupas para crianças na Casa Silvana?
- (d) O que quer comprar a senhora Ferreira?
- (e) De que cor é a blusa que ela experimenta?
- (f) Ela escolhe que cor?

    (g)   Que tipo de sapatos experimenta?

    (h)   Ela gosta ou não?

3   Fill in your part of this dialogue in a grocer's shop.

Senhor Renato	**Bom dia!**
(a) You	*Say hello. I would like a litre of water and a loaf of sliced bread.*
Senhor Renato	**Só temos este pão.**
(b) You	*That's all right. I'll take one. Do you have smoked ham?*
Senhor Renato	**Sim, temos este, que é bom.**
(c) You	*Well, can you cut me six slices please?*
Senhor Renato	**Que mais?**
(d) You	*I also want a tin of peas and a bar of soap.*
Senhor Renato	**Mais?**
(e) You	*That's all thanks. How much is it?*
Senhor Renato	**É um conto, quatrocentos e setenta e cinco se faz favor.**

14

COMER FORA

Eating out

In this unit you will learn

● how to order food in a cafe or restaurant
● something about typical Portuguese food and drink
● how to interpret menus

─────── Diálogo ───────

A pastelaria at the cake shop

Paulo e os amigos entram na pastelaria Suíça.

Empregado	**Boa tarde, que desejam?**
Paulo	**Pois, para mim, um galão e um pastel de bacalhau.**
Nuno	**Eu queria uma bica e uma sandes de queijo.**
Empregado	**E para a menina?**
Maria	**Tem pastéis de nata?**
Empregado	**Temos, sim.**
Maria	**Então dê-me dois, se faz favor.**
Empregado	**E para beber?**
Maria	**Um sumo de laranja.**

Empregado	**Mais alguma coisa?**
Paulo	**Pode ser também um quarto de água mineral.**
Empregado	**Com ou sem gás?**
Paulo	**Sem, e fresca. Obrigado.**
Empregado	**Muito bem.**

a pastelaria *cafe/cake shop*	**um sumo de laranja** *fresh orange juice*
um galão *milky coffee*	
um pastel de bacalhau *cod/potato fish cake*	**mais alguma coisa?** *anything else?*
	um quarto *¼ litre bottle*
uma bica *small black coffee*	**com** *with*
uma sandes *sandwich*	**sem** *without*
pastéis de nata *custard cakes*	**fresca** *cooled*

Comentário

Café *coffee*

In Portugal there are many types of coffee – from small and black, to large and milky, with dozens in between! To ensure you get the better quality coffee, and not the re-cycled beans, ask for **café 'de máquina'**. Here are some of the most popular coffee drinks.

uma bica/um café *small black espresso*	**um pingado/um pingo** *small with one drop of milk*
uma italiana *same but only half-full (very strong)*	**um cafe com leite/uma meia de leite** *white, normal size*
um garoto *small white*	**um galão** *milky (served in a glass)*

 ———————— **Actividades** ————————

1 The waiter has brought a tray of snacks and drinks to the table but has forgotten who ordered what. Can you help him to sort it out?

3 bicas   1 pingado   1 galão
1 sandes de queijo   4 pastéis de bacalhau   5 pastéis de nata
3 sandes de fiambre

What would each person ask for?

(a) Paulo wants a black coffee, ham sandwich and custard cake.
(b) Nuno wants a milky coffee, cheese sandwich, cod cake and custard cake.
(c) Ana wants a black coffee, ham sandwich and 2 cod cakes.
(d) Maria wants a small slightly milky coffee, ham sandwich and 2 custard cakes.
(e) Miguel wants a black coffee, 1 cod cake and 1 custard cake.

BANNER'S

PREPARAMOS ANIVERSÁRIOS

TAKE AWAY
Telef. 86 20 42

Noite do Estudante
A partir das 20H00
20% Desconto
Segunda Feira

RUA BRAAMCAMP, 62

COMIDA RÁPIDA DE LISBOA – SOC. GESTÃO HOTELEIRA, LDA.
Contribuinte N.º 500 236 157
RESTAURANTE 2ª CLASSE

PIZZAS

SEXTAS,SÁBADOS E VÉSPERAS DE FERIADOS
ABERTO ATÉ ÀS 02 HORAS DA MADRUGADA

ABERTO TODOS OS DIAS DAS 11.30H ÀS 24.00H

		PEQUENA	MÉDIA	FAMILIAR
1) MARGARITA	Molho de tomate, queijo, orégão	590$	1.080$	1.425$
2) FANTASIA	Salame	880$	1.445$	2.110$
3) ROMANA	Anchovas, ovo, fiambre	880$	1.445$	2.110$
4) VEGETARIANA	Pimentos verdes, cogumelos, cebola	880$	1.445$	2.110$
5) RAINHA	Fiambre, cogumelos, tomate	960$	1.585$	2.300$
6) MAFIOSO	Salame, pimentos verdes, cebola	1.050$	1.735$	2.520$
7) EXÓTICA	Ananás, fiambre	1.050$	1.735$	2.520$
8) QUATRO ESTAÇÕES	Salame, fiambre, cogumelos, azeitonas, ovo	1.120$	1.835$	2.690$
9) NEPTUNO	Camarão, mexilhão, berbigão, azeitonas	1.120$	1.835$	2.690$
10) FRANGO	Frango, cogumelos, azeitonas	1.120$	1.835$	2.690$
11) MEXICALE	Feijão, piri piri, tomate, alface, carne picada	1.120$	1.835$	2.690$
12) BANNER'S	Salame, cogumelos, pimentos verdes, fiambre, pepperoni, cebola	1.250$	2.035$	2.980$
13) CALZONE	Qualquer Pizza (de cima), fechada			

Diálogo

Nuno e Miguel estão com pressa e querem comer alguma coisa rápida.

Nuno	**Então, o que vais escolher?**
Miguel	**Bom, para mim, acho que quero uma pizza Romana, com uma dose de batatas fritas.**
Nuno	**Tens muita fome! Eu só quero uma pizza Frango, e mais nada.**
Miguel	**Não bebes nada?**
Nuno	**Vou pedir uma pepsi. E tu, o que queres?**
Miguel	**Pois, eu também quero um refrigerante. Talvez uma 7 Up.**
Nuno	**Está bom, então vamos pedir, se não, vamos chegar atrasados ao cinema.**
Empregado	**Façam favor?**
Miguel	**É uma pizza Romana com batatas fritas, uma pizza Frango, uma pepsi e uma 7-Up, se faz favor.**
Empregado	**É para levar, ou vão comer aqui dentro?**
Miguel	**É para comer aqui. Obrigado.**

acho que *I think that*	**um refrigerante** *soft drink*
uma dose *a portion*	**pedir** *to ask for/order*
fome *hunger*	**para levar** *to take out/away*
e mais nada *and nothing else*	

Actividades

2 Look again at the menu on page 130. Which pizzas would you ask for if you wanted the following toppings?

(a) chicken/mushrooms/olives
(b) pineapple/ham
(c) a pizza with lettuce on it
(d) one with egg and mushrooms
(e) one with shrimps

3a (a) When is the place open?
(b) At what times?
(c) Does it give discounts?

3b (a) Ask your friend what they're having.

(b) Say that you think you'll have a chicken pizza.

(c) Tell your friend he/she is hungry.

(d) Ask your friend if they're not drinking anything.

(e) Say you'll ask for a lemonade (7-Up).

(f) Ask your friend if they want a soft drink.

(g) Say you want a portion of chips.

Comentário

Eating and drinking out

There are plenty of places in Portugal where you can eat and drink. If you just want a snack, go to a café or café-bar or **pastelaria** (where cakes abound). For main meals you could choose from the **restaurante**, some of these are graded by a 'star' system, others have their own fame, or there are the **tascas** – usually more reasonably priced and, up to recently, only frequented by men – here you can buy drink straight from the barrel. It's worth asking around to find a **tasca** with a good reputation. Other eating places may have obscure names and you'll only find them by talking to locals.

Drinks

Beer (**cerveja**) is really like the lager drunk in the UK, and if you are accustomed to imported lager such as the Spanish San Miguel, Portuguese beers such as Sagres and, Superbock are very similar. Ask for **uma imperial** for draught Portuguese beer and **uma caneca** for a pint glass. Wine is the thing to drink in Portugal, as it is cheap and in the main, excellent quality.

vinho branco *white wine*	**vinho verde tinto** *red 'green' wine*
vinho tinto *red*	**vinho rosé** *rosé*
vinho verde *'green' wine*	**vinho do Porto** *port wine*

Documento 16

What drinks did these people have with their meal?

RESTAURANTE **Floresta**
CAFÉ
CERVEJARIA **da Cidade**

Contribuinte n.º 805 595 570

Travessa Poço da Cidade, 10-12 – 1200 Lisboa
Telef. 346 06 21

TALÃO DE MESA

Couvert	540$00
Aperitivos . . .	450$00
Sopa	$
Peixe	$
Carne	2200$00
Marisco	$
Pão	160$00
Vinho	1240$00
Águas	150$00
Refrigerantes . . .	$
Cerveja	$

Leitura

A comida portuguesa. See how much of this you understand. Listen to it on the cassette a few times.

A comida portuguesa é muito variada e deliciosa. Cada região tem os seus próprios pratos típicos como, por exemplo, as tripas no Porto; a carne de porco à Alentejana, no Alentejo; e em Trás-os-Montes, a feijoada. Os portugueses comem muito peixe, como as sardinhas (assadas), o bacalhau – dizem que existem 365 receitas para o bacalhau, uma para cada dia do ano! Os mariscos comem-se bastante, em pratos como arroz de marisco, e açorda de marisco. As sopas portuguesas são realmente uma delícia, espessas e muito saudáveis. Experimente o caldo verde. Há sempre pão com as refeições, caseiro, e muito bom. Usa-se muito alho e azeite na cozinha portuguesa, e muito sal – e é por isso que é aconselhável beber bastante água. Os portugueses adoram doces e sobremesas como pudim flan, mousse de chocolate, e outros com nomes estranhos, como papos de anjo, feitos com muitos ovos e açucar que acabam com a dieta!

O vinho é especialmente bom. Há várias regiões que produzem vinho de alta qualidade.

O Douro	a região do vinho do Porto, tanto branco como tinto, e o vinho verde.
Lisboa	sobretudo, em Colares, um bom tinto.
Setúbal	o vinho doce, para sobremesa.
o Alentejo	pequenas cidades como Borba, Redondo, produzem excelentes tintos, de preço baixo.

a comida *food, cuisine*		**espessas e muito saudáveis** *thick and very healthy*	
cada *each*			
os seus próprios *their own*		**o caldo verde** *shredded kale soup*	
as tripas *tripe*		**as refeições** *meals*	
a carne de porco à Alentejana *pork and clams*		**pão-caseiro** *home made bread*	
		alho *garlic*	
a feijoada *bean and pork stew*		**azeite** *olive oil*	
sardinhas assadas *grilled sardines*		**é aconselhável** *it's advisable*	
		sobremesas *desserts*	
o bacalhau *salted cod fish*		**pudim flan** *crême caramel*	
os mariscos *seafood*		**acabam com a dieta** *put pay to any diet!*	
arroz de marisco *seafood rice*			
açorda de marisco *seafood/bread mixture*			

—— # A ementa/a lista *the menu* ——

A Ementa/a lista

Entradas	*Starters*
Carne	*Meat*
Peixe	*Fish*
Sobremesas/Doces	*Sweets*
Bebidas	*Drinks*
Vinhos	*Wines*
Couvert	*Cover charge*

Pratos do Dia

costeletas de porco	900$00
escalopes de perú	950$00
bacalhau à Gomes Sá	980$00
arroz de marisco	1,600/760$00
laranja	
mousse	
pudim	

Comentário

Your main menu is divided up as in the first **ementa** above. **Couvert** is a cover charge for bread, butter, and so on. Be careful in some restaurants, especially the more tourist-orientated ones, your table will be laden with plates of olives, cheese, ham, shrimps. These are a real temptation to nibble on, and a pricey one at that. The products are usually expensive, and if you should decide to bite into just one shrimp, eat just one olive, you will be charged for the plateful! The best thing to do is to establish from the outset exactly what you want, and ask them to take the other plates away.

Pratos do dia

The dishes of the day. On the blackboard above, you have been given a choice of pork chops / turkey steaks / bacalhau, or seafood rice. These will usually be served with salad, rice and chips. You will see some dishes have a cheaper price for a **meia dose** = half portion. As Portuguese portions are generally huge, this is an option worth considering. For dessert you have been offered oranges, mousse or crème caramel.

> A ementa turística
> Pão e manteiga
> carne de porco
> ou
> pescada
> mousse de chocolate
> ou
> salada de frutas
> /2 garrafa de vinho/
> refrigerante
> café
> 1,400$00

Ementa turística

The tourist (set) menu, is usually of average value, but offers a complete meal, with drinks, without spending time on lengthy deliberations.

The menu above gives:

bread and butter
pork or hake
chocolate mousse or fruit salad
½ bottle wine/soft drink
coffee

 ——————— **Actividades** ———————

4   Fill in your part of the conversation with the waiter.

	Empregado	**Boa noite. Faz favor.**
(a)	You	*Greet the waiter and ask if there is any soup.*
	Empregado	**Sim, hoje temos sopa de marisco ou caldo verde.**
(b)	You	*Say you'd like a caldo verde.*
	Empregado	**E depois, para comer?**
(c)	You	*Tell him you'd like a half portion of the cod*

dish. *Ask him if there is salad with it.*

Empregado **Sim, vem com uma pequena salada mista.**

(d) You *Say that's OK.*

Empregado **E para sobremesa?**

(e) You *Say you'll have the crème caramel.*

Empregado **E para beber?**

(f) You *Tell him you'll have half a bottle of white wine and a black coffee afterwards.*

5 An inattentive waiter has set out this menu incorrectly. Where should each item appear?

EMENTA

1 carne de porco à Alentejana

2 açorda de marisco

3 pão   A) Entradas

4 vinho da casa

5 queijo da Serra

6 manteiga   B) Carnes

7 salada de frutas

8 café

9 pudim Molotov C) Peixes

10 sopa de legumes

11 refrigerantes

12 bolo de chocolate D) Sobremesas

13 caldo verde

14 prato de camarão

15 bacalhau à Brás E) Bebidas

16 escalopes de perú

17 cerveja – imperial

18 pescada

19 mousse de chocolate F) Couvert

20 água mineral

15
SENTIR-SE MAL

Feeling ill

In this unit you will learn

- how to talk about minor ailments and remedies
- how to discuss illness
- how to cope with accidents and hospitals
- how to deal with the chemist and doctor

Antes de começar

If you do have the misfortune to fall ill while in Portugal, and your ailment is only minor, you should go to the chemist (**a farmácia**). Portuguese pharmacists are usually extremely helpful, and will give advice on any problem so that you may not need to go to see a doctor (**um médico**). Consultations have to be paid for. You may go to a local health centre (**centro de saúde**) or the hospital (**o hospital**) if the problem is serious. Treatment at the dentist (**o dentista**) is expensive.

Para estudar

Be prepared for dealing with medical problems by learning some of the following basic language. In general, if a part of the body hurts, you say: **dói-me** (or **doem-me** in the plural), plus the part of the body that hurts.

Dói-me a cabeça.	*My head hurts.*
Doem-me os dentes.	*My teeth hurt.*

You can also say: Tenho uma dor de + part of the body.

Tenho uma dor de garganta.   *I have a sore throat.*

If you are reporting on someone else's problem, the expressions become:

Dói-lhe . . . .   *His / her . . . . hurts.*
Doem-lhe . . . .   *His / her . . . . hurt.*

And:

(Ele) tem . . . .   *(He) has . . . .*
(Ela) tem . . . .   *(She) has . . . .*

In these circumstances you might well need the names of family members, if you want to say *my husband*, *son*, etc and so on. Why not revise unit 4 now so that you're prepared for the exercises in this unit?

Look at this body (**o corpo**), for other parts of the body, and note that you do not say *my* head hurts, but simply *the* head. For sore ears you say **doem-me os ouvidos**, and not **orelhas**.

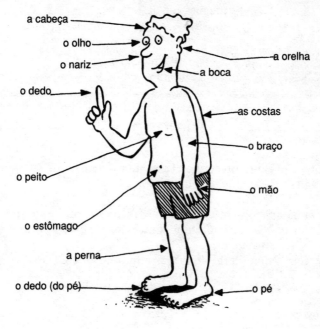

a cabeça
o olho
o nariz
a orelha
a boca
o dedo
as costas
o braço
o peito
o mão
o estômago
a perna
o dedo (do pé)
o pé

Other problems you might need to report include:

estou constipado/a *I have a cold*	**Cortei (cortou)** . . . *I've (he's,*
tenho gripe *I have a cold*	*she's) cut . . .*
tenho uma insolação *I have*	**bati (bateu)** . . . *I've (he's, she's)*
sunstroke	*banged . . .*
tenho uma enxaqueca *I have*	**magoei (magoou)** . . . *I've (he's,*
migraine	*she's) hurt . . .*

———————— Diálogo ————————

João	**Olá Maria, estás bem?**
Maria	**Não, não estou. Tenho uma dor de cabeça.**
João	**Tomaste um remédio?**
Maria	**Sim, tomei uma aspirina há meia hora.**
João	**Então, porque não te vais deitar um pouquinho – vais sentir-te melhor depois.**
Maria	**Tens razão. Vou já para casa.**

tomaste . . . ? *have you taken . . . ?*	**porque não te vais deitar** *why*
um remédio *medicine*	*don't you go and lie down*
tomei *I've taken (I took)*	**um pouquinho** *a little bit*
uma aspirina *you're right*	**sentir-te** *to feel*
há meia hora *½ hr ago*	**vou já** *I'm going right now*

———————— Diálogo ————————

Ana	**Bom dia senhor Carvalho. Como está?**
Sr. Carvalho	**Não me sinto bem.**
Ana	**Qual é o problema?**
Sr. Carvalho	**Sinto-me tonto e creio que vou vomitar.**
Ana	**Não era melhor sentar-se um pouco antes que desmaiar?**
Sr. Carvalho	**Boa ideia. Vou ficar aqui uns momentos.**

não me sinto bem *I don't feel well*	**não era melhor . . . ?** *wouldn't it be*
o problema *problem*	*better . . . ?*
sinto-me tonto *I feel dizzy*	**sentar se** *to sit down*
creio que *I think that*	**desmaiar** *to faint*
vomitar *to be sick*	

Actividade

1 How would you say the following?

   (a) I have a sore throat.
   (b) My daughter has cut her finger.
   (c) My ears hurt.
   (d) My husband has sunstroke.
   (e) I think my son is going to be sick.
   (f) I've banged my toe.
   (g) My friend has hurt her leg.

Comentário

If you are involved in, or need to report, an accident in Portugal, the following information is vital:

Telephone number 115 gets through to the emergency services.

> **Houve um accidente.** *There's been an accident.*
> **Precisamos duma ambulância.** *We need an ambulance.*
>
> **Precisamos de ajuda.** *We need help.*

Be prepared to give details:

> **onde?** *where?*
> **pessoas feridas?** *injured people?*
>
> **o seu nome** *your name*

Speaking on the phone is a daunting task, especially in a situation like this, so try to keep calm, and don't forget useful phrases like:

> **Por favor fale mais devagar.** *Please speak more slowly.*
>
> **Pode repetir?** *Can you repeat?*
> **Sou inglês/inglesa.** *I am English.*

O hospital in Portugal can be a bewildering experience, as in many cases, standards of efficiency can be below what you may be used to.

You will be looked after, but be prepared for some form-filling.

———————— **Actividade** ————————

2 Would you know how to fill in a form (**uma ficha**) like the one below? See how much you can do before looking at the word box.

> FICHA DE DADOS PESSOAIS – Centro de Saúde –
>
> NOME COMPLETO _____
> IDADE _____
> DATA DE NASCIMENTO _____
> LUGAR DE NASCIMENTO _____
> MORADA _____
> NÚMERO DE TELEFONE _____
> BILHETE DE IDENTIDADE _____
> NÚMERO DE CONTRIBUINTE _____
> EM CASO DE EMERGÊNCIA CONTACTAR –

nome completo *full name*
idade *age*
data de nascimento *date of birth*
lugar de nascimento *place of birth*
morada *address*
número de telefone *telephone number*
bilhete de identidade *identity card number (or passport for tourists)*

número de contribuinte *national insurance number (put personal insurance details if known)*
em caso de emergência, contactar . . . *in case of emergency, contact . . .*

Diálogo

Na farmácia at the chemist's

Senhora	**Tem alguma coisa para dor de garganta?**
Farmacêutico	**É para si ou para uma criança?**
Senhora	**Para mim.**
Farmacêutico	**Só tem dor de garganta, ou tem outros sintomas também?**
Senhora	**Tenho uma dorzinha de cabeça também.**
Farmacêutico	**Bom. Recomendo este xarope para a garganta – tome três vezes por dia. E para a cabeça ou estes comprimidos, ou estas aspirinas.**
Senhora	**Levo os comprimidos.**
Farmacêutico	**Tome dois de seis em seis horas.**

tem alguma coisa para . . . ? *do you have something for . . . ?*	**xarope** *syrup*
para si, mim *for you, me*	**3 vezes por dia** *3 times a day*
criança *child*	**ou . . . ou . . .** *either . . . or . . .*
sintomas *symptoms*	**comprimidos** *pills*
recomendo *I recommend*	**levo** *I'll take*
	de seis em seis horas *every six hours*

Documento número 17

For what part of the body is this medicine being advertised?

Quando a garganta arde e queima... **... a solução é Mebocaína.**

Para estudar

Remédios medicines

The following vocabulary might be useful:

comprimidos	*pills*	**um band-aid/um penso**	
aspirina	many medicines	**rápido** *plaster*	
paracetemol	are known by their	**creme para . . .**	*cream for . . .*
migraleve	brand name	**loção para . . .**	*lotion for . . .*
uma ligadura	*bandage*		

Leitura

Look at the following information on health and emergency contacts, and see if you can answer the questions below.

1 What number would you ring if you needed a doctor urgently?
2 On the Lisbon pharmacy phone lines, for what do you have to pay 300$00 escudos?
3 What is Nº 115?
4 In Viseu, which number would you ring if you wanted the district hospital?
5 Why might you ring Nº 26216?

FARMÁCIAS

LISBOA

Das 22 às 9 horas, chamadas com receitas do dia ou da véspera-50$00.
Chamadas não urgentes-300$00

MÉDICO
DE
URGÊNCIA
☎ 795 06 80

NÚMERO NACIONAL DE SOCORRO

115

VISEU (032)

Bombeiros Municipais - 26216
Bombeiros Voluntários - 26812
Hospital Distrital- 424124
GNR - 421958 e 421585
Brigada de Trânsito - 26637
PSP - 422041
Aeródromo de Viseu - 459849
Electricidade
(Falta de luz e água) - 425175
Serviços Municipalizados - 423112
Rodoviária Beira Litoral - 422822

16
VIAJAR DE CARRO
Travelling by car

In this unit you will learn

- how to deal with cars and travel documents
- how to cope with petrol and service stations
- information on roads and road signs
- how to report accidents and theft

Antes de começar

Driving in Portugal can be somewhat daunting, even for the most experienced of drivers: many roads are awkward to handle, due to bad surfaces and pot holes. Portuguese drivers are notoriously difficult to deal with, and driving rules and regulations are constantly changing. If you hire a car, make sure you always travel with the appropriate documentation, such as current driving licence, insurance, proof of hire and, if you borrow a vehicle from friends, you must have a letter of authorisation to drive it.

 ——————— **Diálogo** ———————

Listen to, then read, the following dialogue.

Miguel pede informações sobre o caminho para a Nazaré. *Michael asks for information about the way to Nazaré.*

Miguel	**Desculpe, este é o caminho certo para a Nazaré?**
Senhora	**Não é exactamente, não. Era melhor seguir por esta estrada até a rotunda, e ali tomar a segunda saída, e seguir por aquele caminho.**
Miguel	**Vai demorar muito?**
Senhora	**Acho que não. A Nazaré fica a oitenta quilómetros daqui, mais ou menos. Se seguir a E.N. 135, vai logo ver os sinais para a Nazaré. É um instantinho.**
Miguel	**Muito obrigado e bom dia.**

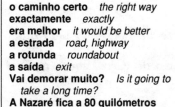

o caminho certo   *the right way*
exactamente   *exactly*
era melhor   *it would be better*
a estrada   *road, highway*
a rotunda   *roundabout*
a saída   *exit*
Vai demorar muito?   *Is it going to take a long time?*
A Nazaré fica a 80 quilómetros daqui.   *Nazaré is 80 kms away.*

Acho que não.   *I don't think so.*
mais ou menos   *more or less*
se seguir   *if you follow*
a E.N. 135 (E.N. = Estrada Nacional)   *national highway (like motorway)*
vai logo ver   *you'll soon see*
os sinais   *road signs*
é um instantinho   *it's really quick*

Para estudar

Study the diagram of a car (**o carro/o automóvel**), and try to learn the names of the various parts. You never know what might make you break down at any time when you are travelling!

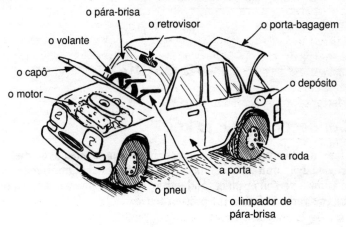

———————— **Diálogo** ————————

Manuela telefona para uma garagem para pedir ajuda. *Manuela telephones a (repair) garage to ask for help.*

Mecánico	**Oficina Oliveira, boa tarde.**
Manuela	**Boa tarde. Faz favor, preciso de ajuda.**
Mecánico	**Qual é o problema?**
Manuela	**O meu carro está avariado. Creio que há um furo num pneu, mas também tive problemas com os travões.**
Mecánico	**Onde está estacionado?**
Manuela	**Estou na E.N. 125, perto de Loulé, ao lado duma escola.**
Mecánico	**Bom, então espere dentro do carro, vou organizar um reboque.**
Manuela	**Vai demorar?**
Mecánico	**Pode demorar um pouco porque não conheço bem o caminho.**
Manuela	**Paciência!**

avariado	*broken down*	**uma escola**	*school*
creio que	*I think, believe that*	**espere**	*wait*
um furo	*puncture*	**organizar**	*organise*
tive problemas	*I've had (some) problems*	**um reboque**	*lift, tow*
os travões	*brakes*	**não conheço bem**	*I don't know well*
estacionado	*parked*	**paciência!**	*patience! (Be patient!)*

 ———————— **Para estudar** ————————

Conhecer, saber to know

There are two verbs in Portuguese that mean *to know* (you met them previously in unit 9). You'll no doubt remember that **conhecer** means to know a person or place, and **saber** means to know a fact. Here are the two verbs in full in the present tense.

	conhecer	**saber**
Eu	conheço	sei
Tu	conheces	sabes
Ele, ela ⎫ você ⎬ o Sr/a Sra ⎭	conhece	sabe
nós	conhecemos	sabemos
eles, elas ⎫ vocês ⎬ os Srs ⎭	conhecem	sabem

Actividade

1 Decide which of the two verbs (**saber/conhecer**) should go in each sentence. The correct form is provided in the brackets to help you.

   (a) A Maria ___ o meu irmão. [sabe/conhece]

   (b) Nós não ___ as horas. [sabemos/conhecemos]

   (c) Tu queres ___ a França? [conhecer/saber]

   (d) Eles ___ o Presidente. [sabem/conhecem]

   (e) O João não ___ o meu nome. [conhece/sabe]

Documento número 18

Why might this particular car be worth a second look?

carro do ano
Troféu **94**
Volante de Cristal

Diálogo

O senhor Neto quer comprar gasolina. *Mr Neto wants to buy some petrol.*

Senhor Neto	**Boa tarde. Quero gasolina se faz favor.**
Attendant	**Claro. Quer super, normal, sem chumbo ou gasóleo?**
Senhor Neto	**Normal**
Attendant	**Quantos litros?**
Senhor Neto	**Pode encher o depósito. Preciso também pôr ar nos pneus, e quero dois litros de óleo por favor.**
Attendant	**Muito bem.**
Senhor Neto	**Aceita cartões de crédito?**
Attendant	**Aceitamos, sim.**

gasolina – super/normal petrol – 4-star/2-star	fill the tank		
sem-chumbo unleaded petrol	**pôr** to put		
gasóleo, óleo diesel, oil	**ar** air		
quantos litros? how many litres?	**aceita/aceitamos** (you) accept/we accept		
pode encher o depósito you can	**cartões de crédito** credit cards		

Actividade

2 See how many of the following you can do.

   (a) Ask if this is the correct way to Lisbon.
   (b) Ask if it's going to take a long time.
   (c) Say that your car is broken down.
   (d) Say that you need a tow.
   (e) Say that you want 8 litres of unleaded petrol.
   (f) Ask if someone accepts credit cards.
   (g) Tell someone to fill the tank up.

Leitura

Read the following passage on driving regulations in Portugal, and see how much of it you can understand.

Conduzir em Portugal: Umas regras gerais

- É obrigatório usar cintos de segurança fora das cidades; crianças menores de 12 anos devem viajar no banco traseiro.

- O limite aceitável (e legal) de álcool é de menos de 0.5 gramas por litro. Apesar da grande campanha contra 'o beber' e 'o conduzir' ('Bebeu? Não conduza!'), é de surpreender quantas pessoas continuam a sair para tomar uns copos, e voltarem para casa de carro.

- Todos os veículos devem ter uma caixa de Pronto-Socorros, e um triângulo vermelho para montar na estrada no caso de avaria.

- Os limites de velocidade – 60 quilómetros por hora dentro de cidades/90 q.p.h. nas estradas/120 q.p.h. nas auto-estradas. Para veículos maiores, tais como camiões e camionetas, os limites chegam a ser aproximadamente 20 por cento mais baixos.

- Se há menos de um ano que se conduz, deve-se observar um limite de velocidade de 90 quilómetros por hora, e deve-se expor um autocolante no vidro traseiro do carro.

---

cintos de segurança *safety-belts*
fora *outside*
deve/devem/deve-se *must*
banco traseiro *back seat*
o limite aceitável *acceptable limit*
apesar de *in spite of*
conduzir *driving, to drive*
Bebeu? Não conduza! *Have you had a drink? Don't drive!*
surpreender *to surprise*
tomar uns copos *to have a few drinks*
uma caixa de Pronto-Socorros *first-aid box*
montar *to erect*

no caso de *in the event of*
avaria *break-down*
tais como *such as*
camiões e camionetas *lorries and coaches*
chegam a ser *come to be/are*
mais baixos *lower*
há menos de um ano *it's less than a year*
um autocolante *a special sticker*
o vidro traseiro *back window*

Actividade

3 Can you answer these questions in Portuguese?

    (a) Onde é obrigatório usar cintos de segurança?
    (b) Todos os veículos devem ter o quê?
    (c) É legal beber e conduzir em Portugal?
    (d) Se está a conduzir há menos de um ano, o que deve fazer?
    (e) Qual é o limite de velocidade para carros nas auto-estradas?

Comentário

If you are involved in a traffic accident, follow the instructions for getting help in Unit 15. You will also need to fill in all kinds of forms, and give a statement to the traffic police (usually the GNR – Guarda Nacional Republicana).

If you experience theft from your vehicle, you will need to report it at the local **Esquadra da Polícia** (*police station*). Dealing with the police in Portugal can be difficult: if you can find someone to go with you, it will certainly help.

Diálogo

A senhora Johnson informa a Polícia sobre um roubo. *Mrs. Johnson reports a theft to the police.*

Senhora Johnson	**Bom dia. Chamo-me Sylvia Johnson e sou inglesa. Estou aqui de férias. Quero comunicar um roubo dalgumas coisas no meu carro.**
Polícia	**Que coisas?**
Senhora Johnson	**A minha máquina fotográfica, uma mala que continha o meu passaporte e carteira com dinheiro.**
Polícia	**Como aconteceu?**
Senhora Johnson	**O vidro está partido.**
Polícia	**A senhora não sabe que corre um grande risco, deixar objectos dentro dum carro?**

Senhora Johnson **Eu sei, mas só demorei um pouco.**
Polícia   **Vai ter de preencher esta ficha em triplic**
                 do. Tem os seus documentos?

comunicar *to report*	**partido** *broken*
um roubo *theft*	**corre um grande risco** *you run a big risk*
que coisas? *which things?*	
a máquina fotográfica *camera*	**deixar** *to leave/leaving*
uma mala que continha . . . *a bag which contained . . .*	**objectos** *objects*
	só demorei um pouco *I was only a little while*
o passaporte *passport*	
a carteira *purse, wallet*	**preencher** *to fill in*
dinheiro *money*	**ficha** *form*
como aconteceu? *how did it happen?*	**em triplicado** *in triplicate*

———— Actividade ————

4 There are eight words connected with cars hidden in this wordsearch. Can you find them?

P	N	E	U	F	V	S	Q	S	G
F	E	U	Q	P	B	E	R	E	A
O	U	N	J	K	W	A	E	O	S
T	C	B	Y	I	D	V	P	V	O
I	B	M	L	A	W	A	P	A	L
S	L	P	R	F	B	R	J	R	I
O	M	T	D	L	M	I	G	T	N
P	S	M	K	B	T	A	J	T	A
E	G	H	Q	A	P	D	C	X	W
D	M	K	Y	W	Q	O	E	L	O

17
ALOJAMENTO
Accommodation

In this unit you will learn

- how to find lodgings
- how to book accommodation
- what to do when things don't work

Listen to, and read through, the following short dialogues relating to hotel accommodation.

 ─────── **Diálogos** ───────

A família Santos procura quartos num hotel. *The Santos family look for rooms in a hotel.*

Senhor Santos	**Tem quartos vagos para hoje?**
Recepcionista	**Temos, sim. Quantos são?**
Senhor Santos	**Somos cinco.**
Recepcionista	**É para quantas noites?**
Senhor Santos	**Vamos ficar cinco noites.**
Recepcionista	**Querem um quarto de família ou quartos individuais?**
Senhor Santos	**O quarto de família tem quantas camas?**
Recepcionista	**Tem uma cama de casal e três camas individuais.**

Senhor Santos	**Qual é o preço?**
Recepcionista	**Seis mil, oitocentos por noite, incluindo o pequeno almoço.**
Senhor Santos	**Então, ficamos com este.**

tem quartos vagos?	*do you have any rooms free?*	**quartos individuais**	*single rooms*
quantos são?	*how many of you are there?*	**cama de casal**	*double bed*
		camas individuais	*single beds*
somos cinco	*there are 5 of us*	**o preço**	*the price*
para quantas noites?	*for how many nights?*	**por noite**	*per night*
		incluindo	*including*
ficar	*to stay*	**ficamos com este**	*we'll have this one*
um quarto de família	*a family room*		

Sonia encontra um problema. *Sonia comes across a problem.*

Sonia	**Tem quartos vagos?**
Recepcionista	**Para quantas pessoas?**
Sonia	**Só para uma.**
Recepcionista	**Para quando?**
Sonia	**Para hoje e amanhã.**
Recepcionista	**Lamento, mas já não há quartos individuais para hoje. Talvez haja no hotel Sol, que fica aqui em frente.**
Sonia	**Está bem. Obrigada pela ajuda.**

para quantas pessoas?	*for how many people?*	**já não há**	*there are no longer*
para quando?	*for when?*	**talvez haja**	*perhaps there may be*
lamento	*I'm sorry*	**obrigada pela ajuda**	*thanks for the help*

A senhora Jones quer reservar um quarto. *Mrs. Jones wants to book a room.*

Senhora Jones	**Está?**
Recepcionista	**Estou, sim.**
Senhora Jones	**É da pensão Lusa?**
Recepcionista	**É sim. Bom dia.**
Senhora Jones	**Olá bom dia. Queria reservar um quarto de casal para o dia 22.**
Recepcionista	**Quantas noites pretendem ficar?**

Senhora Jones	**Três.**
Recepcionista	**Quer com casa de banho privativa?**
Senhora Jones	**Sim se faz favor, e pequeno almoço.**
Recepcionista	**Qual é o nome?**
Senhora Jones	**É Jones.**
Recepcionista	**Como se escreve?**
Senhora Jones	**J–O–N–E–S**
Recepcionista	**Muito bem senhora Jones. Está reservado. Até ao dia 22. Bom dia, com licença.**

está? *hello (on the phone – lit "are you"?)*	**casa de banho privativa** *en-suite bathroom*
estou *hello (on the phone – lit "I am")*	**como se escreve?** *how do you write it?*
a pensão *guest house*	**reservado** *reserved*
reservar *to reserve*	**com licença** *excuse me (to end phone conversation)*
um quarto de casal *a double room*	
pretendem *you (pl) intend, want*	

Actividade

1 How would you do the following:

    (a) Ask if there were rooms free?

    (b) Say there are three of you?

    (c) Say you'd like to reserve a single room?

    (d) Ask if that's the Pensão Sol?

    (e) Ask how much it is with breakfast?

 ——————— **Para estudar** ———————

Hotel talk

um quarto *a room*	**um quarto de casal** *double room*
um quarto individual/simples *single room*	**com cama de casal** *with double bed*
um quarto duplo *double/twin room*	**com duas camas** *with twin beds*

Diálogo

Senhor Green tem um quarto reservado. *Mr Green has a room booked.*

Senhor Green	**Boa noite. Tenho um quarto reservado para hoje e amanhã.**
Recepcionista	**Em que nome?**
Senhor Green	**Green. GREEN**
Recepcionista	**Aqui está, senhor Green. É o quarto trezentos e vinte e cinco. Fica no terceiro andar; o elevador é ali à direita.**
Senhor Green	**Tem uma vista bonita?**
Recepcionista	**Tem, sim. O quarto dá para o mar. Faça favor de preencher esta ficha. Preciso de ficar com o seu passaporte.**

o elevador *lift*	**preencher** *to fill in*
uma vista bonita *a lovely view*	**ficha** *form*
o quarto dá para o mar *the room overlooks the sea*	**preciso** *I need*
	ficar com *to keep*
faça favor de ... *please ... (+ verb).*	**o passaporte** *passport*

Documento número

(a) How many people was this room for?

(b) How much extra was breakfast?

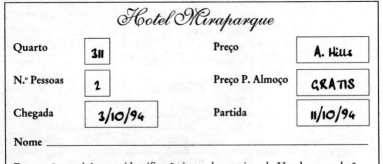

Hotel Miraparque

Quarto	**311**	Preço	**A. Hills**
N.º Pessoas	**2**	Preço P. Almoço	**GRATIS**
Chegada	**3/10/94**	Partida	**11/10/94**

Nome _____

Este cartão servirá para a identificação junto dos serviços do Hotel, que poderão exigir a sua apresentação; Conserve este cartão para utilizar no caso de reclamação perante os Serviços Oficiais de Turismo.

AV. SIDÓNIO PAIS, 12 - LISBOA - PORTUGAL - TEL. 57 80 70 - FAX 57 89 20 - TELEX 16745 - MITEL P

Comentário

There is a variety of accommodation available in Portugal, serving the needs and finance of everybody. You could stay in a **pousada de juventude** (*youth hostel*) if you are on a budget, or for a bit extra, try **a pensão** or **residencial** (*guest house*), where you can usually just get bed and breakfast.

Hotels, like everywhere, range from one to five stars. There is also the **estalagem** or **albergue** (*inn*), and for those who want to splash out a little bit more, the state-run system of **pousadas** – converted castles, monasteries, and stately homes. Wherever you go, you will receive the famous Portuguese welcome.

Diálogo

Quando as coisas não funcionam . . . *When things don't work . . .*

Laura	**Desculpe, o aquecimento no quarto não está a funcionar bem.**
Recepcionista	**Qual é o número do quarto?**
Laura	**É o duzentos e quinze. É possível alguém vir dar uma vista de olhos?**
Recepcionista	**Claro. Peço desculpas. Hoje temos tido alguns problemas. Como vê, o ascensor também está avariado. Creio que é por causa da corte de electricidade que tivemos ontem à noite. Vou ver se podemos arranjar qualquer coisa, está bem?**
Laura	**Obrigada.**

o aquecimento	*the heating*	**temos tido**	*we've been having*
funcionar	*to work*	**como vê**	*as you can see*
não está a funcionar bem	*isn't working well*	**o ascensor**	*lift*
		por causa de	*because of*
alguém	*someone*	**o corte de electricidade**	*power cut*
dar uma vista de olhos	*to have a look*	**tivemos**	*we had*
		ontem à noite	*last night*
peço desculpas	*I'm sorry*	**arranjar**	*to arrange*

Para estudar

More verb forms

- Estar + a + verb, in the present tense, conveys an action that is actually in the middle of being carried out. You can use any person with any verb:

estou a falar	*I am speaking (now)*
estamos a pensar	*we are thinking*

- The simple past tense of **ter** (*to have*) is as follows:

(eu)	tive	*I had, have had*
(tu)	tiveste	*you had, have had*
(ele, ela/você)	teve	*he/she/you had, have had*
(nós)	tivemos	*we had/have had*
(eles, elas)	tiveram	*they/you had/have had*

Talking about actions in the past is fairly complex, and in this course you have only met a few examples.

- To talk about an action that has been happening on a regular, or recent, basis, and still continuing to the present point in time, you need the following structure: **ter** (present tense) + past participle of verb.

Past participles are formed as follows:

-**ar** verbs: falar   falado
-**er** verbs: comer   comido
-**ir** verbs: partir   partido

Remember, there are many irregular verbs which you will pick up in your later studies.

Tenho comprado muitas coisas.   *I've been buying many things.*
O João tem visitado muitos   *John has been visiting many*
   museus.   *museums.*

 —————————— **Actividade** ——————————

2 Can you match up these statements about things that are not working properly?

   (i) O elevador está avariado.   (a) *The cooker doesn't work.*
   (ii) A água não está a funcionar.   (b) *The lift has broken down.*
   (iii) O fogão não funciona.   (c) *The lock isn't working well.*
   (iv) A fechadura não está a   (d) *The water isn't working.*
        funcionar bem.
   (v) O ar condicionado está   (e) *The air-conditioning has*
       avariado.   *broken down.*

Leitura

Read this text on Pousadas, just to get the gist of it, and try to answer the questions.

POUSADAS DE PORTUGAL

Situadas em locais de rara beleza, as Pousadas de Portugal oferecem ao visitante amigo 32 destinos para descobrir as tradições e hábitos das gentes de Portugal.

Côm reduzida capacidade de alojamento, permitem um acolhimento atento e um serviço personalizado.

No campo gastronómico, as Pousadas desvendam-nos os segredos de uma arte milenária recriando o melhor da cozinha regional, acompanhada pelos mais genuínos vinhos portugueses.

Na tranquilidade das Pousadas de Portugal, descobrirá a maneira de viver e o sentir das cidades e aldeias deste país, restituindo-lhe o sentido da arte e do prazer de viajar.

1 How many different destinations are there to choose from?
2 What kind of service is offered?
3 What type of food is offered?
4 What does the tranquility of the Pousadas offer the visitor?
5 Where are the Pousadas situated?

—————— **Actividade** ——————

3 Can you complete your part of this dialogue in a hotel?

   (*a*) You   *Ask if they have rooms free for today.*
        Recepcionista **Temos sim. Quantos são?**
   (*b*) You   *Say there are three of you.*
        Recepcionista **É para quantas noites?**
   (*c*) You   *Say you're going to stay two nights.*
        Recepcionista **Querem quartos individuais?**
   (*d*) You   *Say you would like one double room and one single room.*
        Recepcionista **Querem com casa de banho privativa?**
   (*e*) You   *Say yes please; what is the price?*
        Recepcionista **Quatro mil por pessoa por noite, incluindo o pequeno almoço.**
   (*f*) You   *Say OK, thanks.*

18
FAZER CAMPISMO
Camping

In this unit you will learn

- all about campsites in Portugal
- how to discuss the weather
- how to interpret weather forecasts

Antes de começar

Camping and caravanning in Portugal is popular and cheap, and there are numerous campsites (**parques de campismo**) to choose from, all over the country. Overnight parking in unofficial places is frowned upon.

Diálogo

Listen to, then read, the following extended dialogue a couple of times until the phrases become more familiar to you.

Senhor de Sousa	**Olá bom dia. Tem vagas?**
Recepcionista	**Temos algumas. Tem tendas, carro e caravana ou carrocama?**
Senhor de Sousa	**Temos carro e atrelado com duas tendas.**

Recepcionista	**Bom, temos vários lugares, há um à esquerda debaixo das árvores, outro ao fundo do parque, que dá para o lago, e há dois aqui ao pé do parque infantil.**
Senhor de Sousa	**Qual recomenda?**
Recepcionista	**Pois, é difícil. Aqui, perto do parque infantil é sempre mais barulhento; ao fundo do parque é sossegado, mas um pouco isolado, e debaixo das árvores pois não sei se vai chover hoje, e assim, é uma maçada ter a chuva a pingar em cima das tendas.**
Senhor de Sousa	**Vamos para o fundo. Gostamos do sossego. Qual é o preço?**
Recepcionista	**É mil, seiscentos por pessoa por noite. Vão ficar quanto tempo?**
Senhor de Sousa	**Se calhar, oito dias. Há uma loja aqui no parque?**
Recepcionista	**Aqui ao lado da recepção. Vende tudo, desde mercearias e jornais até garrafas de gás, e coberturas impermeáveis. Abre das 7.30 da manhã até às 9 e quinze da noite. Também há um bar e um pequeno café.**

vagas	*spaces*	**vai chover**	*it's going to rain*
tendas	*tents*	**assim**	*so*
carro e caravana	*car and caravan*	**é uma maçada**	*it's a pain*
carro-cama	*camper*	**a chuva**	*rain*
atrelado	*trailer*	**pingar**	*to drip*
as árvores	*the trees*	**o sossego**	*the quiet*
o lago	*lake*	**se calhar** (colloquial)	*probably*
o parque infantil	*children's playground*	**a recepção**	*reception*
recomenda (you)	*recommend*	**vende**	*it sells*
difícil	*difficult*	**desde . . . até**	*from . . . to . . .*
barulhento	*noisy*	**mercearias**	*groceries*
sossegado	*quiet*	**coberturas impermeáveis**	*ground sheets*
isolado	*isolated*		

Actividade

1   Can you answer these questions based on the dialogue?

(a) Tem vagas no parque de campismo?
(b) O senhor de Sousa tem caravana?
(c) Qual é a vista ao fundo do parque?
(d) Porque é uma maçada debaixo das árvores?
(e) Onde escolhe (chooses) o senhor?
(f) Quanto tempo vão ficar?
(g) A loja vende que tipo de coisas?
(h) A que horas abre?

Documento número 20

Can you match up the symbols to this camping price list?

TENDA PEQUENA	380$00
TENDA GRANDE	560$00
TENDA GRANDE (+ 6 ᵐ)	900$00
CARAVANA	700$00
CARAVANA (+ 6 ᵐ)	1.050$00
AUTOMÓVEL	450$00
AUTOCARRO	1.500$00
CARRO-CAMA	700$00
CARRO-CAMA (+ 6 ᵐ)	1.050$00

(i)   (ii)

(iii)   (iv)

(v)   (vi)

Para estudar

O tempo the weather

	Hoje *Today*	Amanhã *Tomorrow*
	Faz sol/há sol. *It's sunny*	Vai fazer sol. *It's going to be sunny.*
	Faz calor. Está calor (colloq). Está quente. *It's hot.*	Vai fazer calor. Vai estar quente. *It's going to be hot.*
	Faz vento. Há muito vento. *It's windy.*	Vai fazer vento. Vai haver vento. *It's going to be windy.*
	Está a chover. *It's raining.*	Vai chover. *It's going to rain.*
	Faz frio. Está frio. *It's cold.*	Vai fazer frio. Vai estar frio. *It's going to be cold.*
	Está a nevar. Há neve. *It's snowing.*	Vai haver neve. Vai nevar. *It's going to snow.*

Diálogo

Listen to the following two short dialogues on your cassette, and/or read them. Campers are discussing the weather problems. Then answer the **Verdadeiro/Falso** exercise below.

Manuel   **Ai! Que horror!**
Sofia   **O que há?**
Manuel   **Estou completamente picado pelos mosquitos. Deve ser por causa do calor.**
Sofia   **Olhe aqui também, toda a roupa está cheia de areia. Deve ser o vento.**
Manuel   **Vamos procurar outro lugar.**

Ai! *Ahh!*	**picado** *stung/bitten*
Que horror! *Oh no/how awful!*	**os mosquitos** *mosquitoes*
O que há! *What's the matter?*	**deve ser** *it must be*
What's up?	**cheia de** *full of*
completamente *completely*	**areia** *sand*

Luís   **Ai! Não acredito!**
Tania   **O que há?**
Luís   **Temos um buraco. A água está a pingar dentro da tenda. Toda a roupa está molhada.**
Tania   **Olhe aqui também, a entrada está toda cheia de lama. Deve ser por causa da chuva.**

não acredito *I don't believe it*	**molhada** *wet*
um buraco *leak, hole*	**lama** *mud*

Actividade

2   Say whether these statements, based on the two dialogues above, are **verdadeiro** (v) **ou falso** (f).

(a) A Sofia está picada pelos mosquitos.
(b) A roupa do Manuel está cheia de areia.
(c) É por causa da chuva.

(d) A tenda do Luís tem um buraco.

(e) Há lama dentro da tenda.

(f) É por causa da chuva.

Leitura

Look at this weather picture, and see if you can correctly interpret the text.

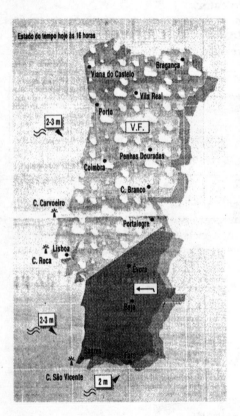

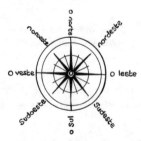

Estado do tempo hoje às 16 horas

Hoje,

No Continente:
Regiões do Norte e Centro: céu pouco nublado; vento fraco do quadrante leste; acentuado arrefecimento nocturno e formação de geada. *Estado do mar:* encrespado; ondulação noroeste de dois a três metros.
Regiões do Sul: céu pouco nublado, temporariamente muito nublado; vento fraco ou moderado de leste. *Estado do mar:* na costa ocidental, mar encrespado; ondulação noroeste de dois a três metros; na costa sul, mar encrespado ou de pequena vaga; ondulação sueste de dois metros.

Amanhã

Céu geralmente limpo; vento fraco ou moderado de leste; acentuado arrefecimento nocturno com formação de geada.

Céu limpo	Céu muito nublado	Trovoadas	V.F. Vento fraco	Vento moderado	Vento forte
Céu pouco nublado	Chuva	Nevoeiro	Neve	Geada	Ondulação

céu limpo *clear sky*	**nevoeiro** *thick fog*
céu pouco nublado *slightly cloudy sky*	**vento fraco** *light wind*
	neve *snow*
céu muito nublado *very cloudy sky*	**vento moderado** *moderate wind*
	geada *frost*
chuva *rain*	**vento forte** *strong wind*
trovoadas *thunder*	**ondulação** *tides*

Say whether these statements are **verdadeiro ou falso**.

1 Hoje no norte o vento está forte.
2 Amanhã em geral o céu vai estar limpo.
3 Hoje, perto de Beja, o vento está moderado.
4 Hoje, no sul, o mar tem uma ondulação de quatro metros.
5 Amanhã vai haver geada à noite.
6 Hoje, no centro, o vento é do sul.

Actividade

3 Match up these weather boxes with the appropriate captions.

(i) Faz frio

(a)

(ii) Há neve.

(b)

(iii) Há sol.

(c)

(iv) Está a chover.

(d)

(v) Faz vento.

(e)

(vi) Há trovoadas.

(f)

4 Fill in the gaps on this table with weather expressions in the present or future tense using the *going to* construction.

Hoje	Amanhã
Faz calor	(a) ___
Há sol.	(b) ___
(c) ___	Vai fazer frio.
Está a chover.	(d) ___
(e) ___	Vai haver vento.
(f) ___	Vai nevar.

19

DIVERTIMENTOS

Distractions

In this unit you will learn

- how to talk about activities on the beach
- how to talk about parks
- how to talk about cultural activities

Diálogo

Jorge e Teresa decidem-se a ir à praia. *George and Theresa decide to go to the beach.*

Jorge   **Vamos à praia hoje?**

Teresa   **Está bem. Faz calor, é ideal para ir nadar. Podemos levar um piquenique, e passar a tarde inteira. Que tal?**

Jorge   **Boa! Podemos jogar volebol.**

Teresa   **Tu podes jogar sozinho, eu quero apanhar sol e dormir!**

Jorge   **Preguiçosa! Cuidado com o sol. É periogoso dormir. Precisamos de levar protecção contra o sol.**

a praia *beach*	**levar** *to take*
é ideal para *it's ideal for*	**um piquenique** *picnic*
nadar *to swim*	**a tarde inteira** *the whole afternoon*
podemos *we can*	**que tal?** *what about (that)!*

boa! (coll.) *great idea!*	**preguiçosa** *lazy*
volebol *volleyball*	**cuidado** *careful*
sozinho *alone*	**é perigoso** *it's dangerous*
apanhar sol *to sunbathe*	**protecção** *protection*
dormir *to sleep*	**contra** *against*

Diálogo

O Senhor Mendes e a Senhora Oliveira falam sobre o que fizeram ontem.
Mr. Mendes and Mrs. Oliveira talk about what they did yesterday.

Senhor Mendes	**O que fez ontem?**
Senhora Oliveira	**Ontem, pois, fui com a minha família ao parque. Foi um dia muito bonito para passear.**
Senhor Mendes	**O que fizeram lá?**
Senhora Oliveira	**Levámos um piquenique, e andámos à sombra das árvores. Os meus filhos jogaram futebol, e vimos muitas coisas – pássaros, flores, e tantas borboletas!**
Senhor Mendes	**Foram ao lago também?**
Senhora Oliveira	**Fomos. Havia muita gente, portanto não conseguimos um barco, mas gostámos muito do passeio. E o senhor, fez alguma coisa interessante?**
Senhor Mendes	**Eu? Trabalhei o dia inteiro!**

o que fez ontem? *what did you (sing.) do yesterday?*	**jogaram** *(they) played*
fui/fomos/foram *I went/we went/you went*	**vimos** *we saw*
foi *it was*	**pássaros, flores** *birds, flowers*
o parque *park*	**tantas** *so many*
passear *to go for a stroll*	**borboletas** *butterflies*
o que fizeram lá? *what did you (pl.) do there?*	**o lago** *lake*
levámos *we took*	**havia muita gente** *there were a lot of people*
andámos *we walked*	**não conseguimos** *we didn't manage (to get)*
à sombra das árvores *in the shade of the trees*	**gostámos** *we liked (enjoyed)*
	trabalhei *I worked*

Para estudar

I came, I saw, I conquered

Talking in the past is a complex matter in Portuguese, and realistically falls outside the realms of this beginner's course. However, below you'll see the verb endings for the three regular verb groups, plus some irregular examples. These are the simple past tense that you use when talking about completed actions.

	-ar FAL/AR (*to speak*) [*spoke*]	**-er** COM/ER (*to eat*) [*ate*]	**-ir** PART/IR (*to leave*) [*left*]
Eu	FALei	COMi	PARTi
Tu	FALaste	COMeste	PARTiste
Ele, ela, você	FALou	COMeu	PARTiu
Nós	FALámos	COMemos	PARTimos
Eles, elas	FALaram	COMeram	PARTiram

	IR (*to go*) [*went*]	FAZER (*to do, make*) [*did, made*]	VER (*to see*) [*saw*]
Eu	fui	fiz	vi
Tu	foste	fizeste	viste
Ele, ela, você	foi	fez	viu
Nós	fomos	fizemos	vimos
Eles, elas	foram	fizeram	viram

Here are some common expressions that are useful when referring to past time.

ontem   *yesterday*
anteontem   *the day before yesterday*
a semana passada   *last week*
o mês passado   *last month*
o ano passado   *last year*

a quinta (feira) passada   *last Thursday*
nas férias passadas   *last holiday*
ontem à noite   *last night*

——————————— **Actividade** ———————————

1a Match up the people on the left, via a verb in the middle, to an activity on the right. In this way you'll be forming complete sentences in the past.

(a)	O Paulo	viste	ao parque.
(b)	Tu	fizeram	o filme.
(c)	Eu e a Maria	foi	ontem.
(d)	Vocês	visitámos	muitas coisas interessantes.
(e)	Eu	trabalhei	a cidade.

1b Can you do the following?

(a) Suggest that you and a friend go to the park today.
(b) Say that you want to play football.
(c) Ask your close friend what they did yesterday.
(d) Say that you went to the beach.
(e) Ask John if he liked the park.

Comentário

There are many things to see and do in Portugal. For example, you can visit some of the loveliest and oldest castles (**castelos**) and palaces (**palácios**) in Europe. There are many areas of outstanding natural beauty including parks, forests (**florestas**), and mountain ranges (**serras**). There are plenty of rich museums (**museus**), churches (**igrejas**) and art galleries (**galerias de arte**) to visit too.

You can participate in sport; tennis, golf, football, and water sports are popular, especially windsurfing. Or you can simply sit at an outdoor café, read a paper, sip a cooling drink, and simply watch the world go by.

——————————— **Leitura** ———————————

Read the following description of a range of holiday activities available to visitors, then look at the exercise below it.

🔭 região de turismo do algarve

1
MERCADOS

*T*udo se compra, tudo se vende. Desde a fresca hortaliça às flores perfumadas. Dos coloridos molins dos muares que puxam as carroças de grandes rodas aos cestos de empreita que têm múltiplas utilizações. E, também, fruta, objectos de uso diário, vestuário, etc.

2
EXPOSIÇÕES

*C*onhecer as obras de artistas portugueses e estrangeiros. Desvendar as tradições, o património cultural do povo algarvio. Uma forma de enriquecer as suas férias.

3
FOLCLORE

A dança algarvia é endiabrada, alegre, rápida. Fala de dias de sol, de corpos ágeis, de tradições que se revivem porque são eternas. E a sua música fica no ouvido...

4
DESPORTO

O sol sempre presente. Clima ameno nos 12 meses do ano. Variado e moderno equipamento. Razões que fazem do Algarve o paraíso dos desportistas.

5
PARQUES DE DIVERSÕES

A alegria e o sol juntam-se para horas de prazer, de puro divertimento. Uma forma sempre agradável de viver dias de férias com toda a família.

6
ACTIVIDADES CULTURAIS

2 **Ciclo de passeios de natureza**
Alcalar e Senhora do Verde
Passeio à descoberta do património natural e arqueológico desta zona do interior rural do concelho de Portimão

7
FADO

*O*uvir o fado é penetrar os segredos da alma portuguesa. Nos sons plangentes da guitarra, no canto que evoca amores e ciúmes, revela o sentido da palavra saudade.
Fado é alegria e tristeza, é música que se ouve em silêncio, é uma recordação que fica para sempre.

You have been handed this leaflet about activities in the Algarve. Each member of your family likes different things. Look at the profiles of your family below for the purpose of this exercise, and decide which activity each member of the family would like the best. Match up the activity or sightseeing venue to the member of the family.

Your family profile

Mother	Likes looking at paintings. Wants to do something cultural, but prefers to be inside.
Father	Is keen on the outdoor life, and has an interest in old ruins, and areas of natural beauty.
Teenage brother	Wants to spend his time out in the sun playing tennis and windsurfing.
Two young sisters	Want to do an activity involving all the family.
Grandparents	Prefer something a bit quieter. Grandad is an enthusiastic guitar player.

 ———————— **Actividade** ————————

2 Complete the dialogue following the English prompts.

Barbara **O que fez a semana passada?**
(a) You *Say that last week you and your sister visited Lisbon.*

Barbara **O que fizeram lá?**
(b) You *Say that you went to a palace, and saw many interesting things.*

Barbara **Levaram um piquenique?**
(c) You *Say no, we ate in a café in the square.*

Barbara **Gostaram da visita?**
(d) You *Say that you both enjoyed it very much.*

20
FINALMENTE
FINALLY

Congratulations, you have come to the end of the course. You have achieved a great deal so far. Learning a language on your own at home is no easy option, but having worked through this course, with the aid of the cassette to improve your listening skills, you should now have enough confidence to try your Portuguese for real. In whichever Portuguese-speaking country you are, the inhabitants will welcome visitors who, like yourself, make an effort to speak the language. A whole new world can open up to you, as you see the faces of Portuguese people light up, and they'll ask, enthusiastically, **Fala português?** You will find that it's well worth the time and effort you have invested.

The Portuguese you have learnt in this course is the 'standard' language you'll hear among average eloquent speakers of the language. However, as you travel around Portugal (or if you visit other Portuguese-speaking countries), you will become aware of regional differences in accent, dialect and vocabulary. For example, the people of the Algarve tend to 'eat' their words a lot more than standard Portuguese speakers. In the Algarve both the beginning and the end of sentences can be muffled, or disappear almost completely, making it quite tricky to decipher. For example the word **escudos** will normally sound like **scuds**. The local expression for a bread roll in the Algarve is **papo-seco**, whereas the standard **pãozinho** is the norm in Lisbon. Don't let this alarm you; imagine a Portuguese person in the UK having to deal with bread roll, bap, barm cake, oven muffin, breakfast roll and so on! In rural areas, the speech is generally more drawn-out and melodic; in one part of the isolated northern regions, an old form of Latin is still found. Be prepared for these differences and don't forget that they exist in every country. Don't be too rigid with what you have learnt so far. You have the best foundations to build on, but you need to be flexible enough to massage and modify as you go along.

As far as learning grammar is concerned, what you have encountered during this course is a basic grounding for simple, everyday conversations. In recent years grammar in language learning has been a taboo subject, but it is now recognised once more that with no grammatical structure learners cannot progress to form their own ideas and responses.

Verbs, of course, are the vital element in any language, and in Portuguese they are perhaps more complex than other Latin languages. In this course you have started talking about actions in the present tense, you have found an easy way of talking about the future, using the verb *to go* and finally you have touched on the structure for one of the past tenses. To progress your learning and to prepare yourself for real conversations with Portuguese people, you now need to follow up with some further studying.

However, the most important thing about learning a language is to have constant contact with it in the spoken and written forms. Obviously the ideal would be to go and immerse yourself in the whole experience of living in Portugal. The next best thing is to discipline yourself to setting aside about ten to fifteen minutes every day to practise. Cassettes, videos, radio, satellite TV all help to improve the skill of listening. Reading is also essential so you could try to get hold of a Portuguese magazine or newspaper and glance through small articles for the gist only. Don't try to read a three page article all at once as you would no doubt soon tire of it and become disillusioned. Bite-sized chunks are what is required. A little and often is the answer to learning. You could think of the process as a mental work-out: would you try to run the marathon on your first day's run?

And so, where to from here? To improve on what you have already taken on board so well, you need a complete course, or, ideally, join a class where you can practise speaking with other people, and have the feedback from a teacher. Whatever you decide to do, remember to enjoy it, and have a great time trying it all out on your travels. **Boa Sorte!**

— KEY TO EXERCISES —

Unit 1
1 está / Estou / bem, obrigada / noite / até / Boa.   2 (*a*) Olá, bom
dia. (*b*) Bom dia (*or* boa tarde *if after midday*). (*c*) Boa tarde, até
amanhã. (*d*) Adeus (*or* Tchau), até logo / até já. (*e*) Olá, boa noite.
3 (*a*) Boa tarde, estou bem obrigado/a. E o Nuno, como está?
(*b*) Adeus (tchau), até amanhã.

Documento 1: Afternoon (**tarde**).

4 (*a*) Como se chama? (*b*) Como te chamas? (*c*) Como se chama
(o senhor)?   5 Bom dia, como está?/Estou bem, obrigado, e a
senhora?/Bem, obrigada./Desculpe, mas como se chama?/Chamo-me
Lúcia, e o senhor?/Eduardo./Muito prazer./Igualmente   6   Boa
tarde/Olá/Bom dia/Adeus/Até logo/Até já.
Avaliação: (*a*) Boa tarde, como está? (*b*) Boa noite, até a próxima.
(*c*) Como te chamas? (*d*) Chamo-me .... (*e*) Desculpe! (*f*) Muito prazer.

Unit 2
1 (*a*) Sou da (Inglaterra). (*b*) Sou (inglês / inglesa). (*c*) De onde
é Senhor Silva? (*d*) A Ana é brasileira. (*e*) De onde são (Sr. e
Senhora Brito)? (*f*) O Paulo é da Itália. (*g*) O Senhor e a Senhora
McDonald são escoceses. 2 (*a*) portuguesa. (*b*) Alemanha,
(*c*) americanas, (*d*) ingleses (*e*) Itália, (*f*) escocês. 3 (*b*) Os
senhores Schmidt são alemães. Eles são da Alemanha. (*c*) A Ellen
e a Mary são dos Estados Unidos. Elas são Americanas.

(*d*) A Sandra, o John e a Brenda são da Inglaterra. Eles são ingleses.
(*e*) O Marco e o Giovanni são italianos. Eles são da Itália. (*f*) O Mac
é da Escócia. Ele é escocês. 4 (*a*) Fala italiano? (*b*) Não sou
americano/a. (*c*) Falo português e inglês. (*d*) Fala português?
(*e*) Não sou alemão/ã, mas falo alemão. 5 (*a*) Falso, (*b*)
Verdadeiro, (*c*) Verdaderio, (*d*) Verdadeiro, (*e*) Falso.
6 (*a*) Sim, falo um pouco. (*b*) Não, não sou alemão/ã, sou
(inglês/a). (*c*) Sim, falo inglês e (também) italiano. (*d*) Obrigado/a,
adeus.

Documento 2a: (*a*) English, (*b*) German, Italian.
2b English, Portuguese, German.

Avaliação: (*a*) De onde é, Paulo? (*b*) Sou da (Inglaterra). (*c*) (o
senhor Mendes) é brasileiro? (*d*) De onde são? (*e*) Somos (ingleses
/ inglesas). (*f*) A Júlia é portuguesa. (*g*) O João é dos Estados
Unidos? (*h*) Fala inglês? (*i*) Não, não falo alemão. (*j*) Sim, sou
inglês / inglesa.

Unit 3
1 (*a*) Onde mora (vive) Senhora Gomes? (*b*) Moro (vivo) na
Inglaterra. (*c*) A Maria mora (vive) na praça. (*d*) Onde moram os
senhores? (*e*) (O Renato) vive na Alemanha? 2 (*a*) A Lúcia mora
na avenida. (*b*) Nós moramos na rua. (*c*) Mora no beco. (*d*) Eles
moram na praça. 3 (*a*) iii, (*b*) iv, (*c*) i, (*d*) ii, (*e*) v.

Documento 3: Pastelaria Antiqua.

4 (*a*) Onde trabalha senhor Gomes? (*b*) Sou estudante.
(*c*) O que faz, José? (*d*) Trabalho num/a .... (*e*) Não trabalho.
5 (*a*) Universidade, (*b*) banco, (*c*) empresa, (*d*) aeroporto,
(*e*) escritório, (*f*) escola. 6 (*a*) cinco, (*b*) doze, (*c*) treze,
(*d*) dezoito, (*e*) dois, (*f*) dezanove.

Avaliação: (*b*) Onde moram os senhores? (*c*) Moro em
(Lancaster). (*d*) Moro numa rua / praça / avenida. (*e*) Moro numa
casa moderna. (*f*) Onde trabalha? (*g*) O que faz? (*h*) Sou
(professora) (*i*) Trabalho numa (escola).

Unit 4
1 (*a*) o meu irmão. (*b*) a nossa mãe. (*c*) a sua filha.
(*d*) os nossos filhos. (*e*) o meu pai. 2 (*a*) A Ana é a filha mais
nova. (*b*) O Miguel é o nosso irmão mais alto. (*c*) Eles são os meus
filhos mais velhos. (*d*) o António é mais baixo. (*e*) a Maria e a
Paula são mais altas. 3 (*a*) Chama-se Rosa. (*b*) Trabalha numa

escola secundária.   (*c*) É o Roberto.   (*d*) É muito calma.
(*e*) Trabalha num hospital.   (*f*) Não, é alto.   4   (*a*) Tem uma filha?
(*b*) Temos dois filhos.   (*c*) Ela tem um irmão?   (*d*) Tenho uma
irmã.   (*e*) Têm filhos?   5   Preguiçoso, elegante, desportivo,
barulhento, sério, calmo, nervoso, honesto.

Documento 4: Age up to 25, not a student, hard-working.

6   Quantos anos tem a sua filha? Ela tem onze anos.

Avaliação: (*a*) Este é o meu marido / esta é a minha mulher.
(*b*) Aquele á o meu irmão / aquela é a minha irmã.   (*c*) Esté é o
nosso filho / esta é a nossa filha   (*d*) Aquela é a minha irmã mais
nova.   (*e*) O meu marido é (sério) /a minha mulher é (honesta) / o
meu professor é (calmo).   (*f*) Sou (encantador).   (*g*) Quantos anos
tem?   (*h*) Tenho (x) anos.

Unit 5
1   (*a*) Os senhores gostam de frango?   (*b*) Não gostas do caldo
verde?   (*c*) Não, não gosto.   (*d*) Gostamos muito (imenso) de
sardinhas.   (*e*) a Paula gosta um pouco de arroz de marisco.
(*f*) Gostam imenso da comida portuguesa.   2   (*a*) a, (*b*) o,   (*c*)
amos,   (*d*) as,   (*e*) am.   3   (*a*) iii,   (*b*) i,   (*c*) v,   (*d*) ii,   (*e*) iv.

Documento 5: Sea-food rice (Arroz de Marisco).

4   (*a*) Sim. Gosta.   (*b*) Porque é um país muito limpo.   (*c*) Porque
tem um clima agradável.   (*d*) Não, não gostam muito.   (*e*) A
mulher do Nuno prefere a Dinamarca.   (*f*) Porque preferem o
barulho.

Documento 6: Something different.

5   (*a*) Prefiro a Inglaterra porque é histórica.   (*b*) O senhor
Antunes prefere a Suiça ou a Dinamarca?   (*c*) A Sonia prefere a
Itália porque é interessante.   (*d*) Qual preferem (os senhores), os
Estados Unidos, ou o Japão?   (*e*) Preferimos a Holanda porque é
bonita.   6   Velho / movimentado / desagradável / caro / sujo / calmo /
limpo.

Avaliação:

(*a*) Gosta de frango?   (*b*) Gosto um pouco de sardinhas.   (*c*) O
Miguel gosta imenso da comida portuguesa.   (*d*) O Senhor não gosta
do caldo verde?   (*e*) Prefiro Portugal porque é interessante.
(*f*) Qual preferem – a Itália ou o Japão?   (*g*) Preferimos a comida
dinamarquesa.

Unit 6

1 (*a*) Ana Maria's, (*b*) Roberto's. 2 típica / três / pequenos / grande / terraço / há / casa de banho / baixo / cozinha / de / sala de jantar. 3 [*Typical answer*]: A minha casa é uma casa moderna. Fica num Bairro moderno. Na casa há dois quartos em cima, e uma cozinha e uma sala de estar em baixo. Gosto da minha casa. 4 (*a*) Em frente da lareira. (*b*) Um vaso de flores. (*c*) Debaixo da mesa. (*d*) Sim, há. (*e*) Um quadro bonito e um armário. (f) Não; há um chuveiro. 5 (*a*) Falso, (*b*) Falso, (*c*) Falso, (*d*) Verdadeiro, (*e*) Falso, (f) Verdadeiro. 6 (*a*) O gato está em cima do frigorífico. (*b*) Há um armário ao lado da estante. (*c*) Há um sofá detrás da mesa? (*d*) O chuveiro não está na cozinha. (*e*) O fogão está ao lado da máquina de lavar. (f) O gato está em frente da poltrona?

Documento 7: (*a*) Three, (*b*) Yes.

Avaliação: (*a*) (e.g.) Tenho um apartamento moderno. (*b*) (e.g.) A minha casa tem . . . uma cozinha . . . . (*c*) Como é a sua casa? (*d*) Tenho uma cozinha / casa de banho grande / pequena. (*e*) Há dois / três / quatro / cinco quartos. (f) Não há uma sala de estar / sala de jantar. (*g*) (e.g.) O sofá está ao lado da mesa. (*h*) (e.g.) O frigorífico está na cozinha. (*i*) O que há no quarto?

Unit 7

1 (*a*) levanta-se, (*b*) 9 horas, (*c*) janta / sete menos um quarto, (*d*) aula de japonês, (*e*) à uma. 2 (*a*) iii, (*b*) vi (*c*) iv, (*d*) i, (*e*) v, (f) ii. 3 (*a*) iii, (*b*) i, (*c*) iv, (*d*) ii, (*e*) v. 4 [Sample answers] (*a*) Levanto-me às 7 horas. (*b*) Almoço ao meio-dia. (*c*) Chego em casa às 5 e meia. (*d*) Deito-me às 10 e um quarto.

Documento 8: Wednesday a.m. (**4ª feira de manhã**)

5 (*a*) Levanto-me cedo. (*b*) Ele não se deita tarde. (*c*) A que horas se vestem? (*d*) Não nos vestimos rápidamente. (*e*) Como se chamam? (f) A que horas te levantas? 6 (*a*) compreende, (*b*) parte, (*c*) comemos, (*d*) vivem, (*e*) sobes, (f) bebe.

Avaliação: (*b*) A que horas se levanta? (*d*) Não nos deitamos até as 10 e meia. (*e*) A que horas almoça nos / aos domingos (Paulo)? (f) Não como muito nas / às terças. (*g*) A que horas vai à igreja Jorge? (*h*) Que horas são?

Unit 8

1 (*a*) Maria, o que gosta de fazer no tempo livre? (*b*) Gosto de costurar. (*c*) Os Senhores gostam de viajar? (*d*) Gostam de practicar desportos? (*e*) (e.g.) Não gosto de dançar. (*g*) Gostas de nadar no tempo livre? 2 (*a*) Sim, claro. (*b*) Não, não somos portugueses, somos ingleses. Somos de . . . (Manchester). (*c*) Sim, falo um pouco de português. (*d*) Gosto de ir ao teatro. (*e*) O meu marido / a minha mulher gosta de trabalhar no jardim, e os meus filhos gostam de practicar desportos. (*f*) Sim, claro!

Documento 9: Yes.

3 livros / leio / dias / vejo / ouve / joga / nunca / lê / gosta / vão / todas / vez / quando / fazem. 4 (*a*) iii, (*b*) vi, (*c*) iv, (*d*) i, (*e*) v, (*f*) ii. 5 (*a*) cada dia, (*b*) uma vez por mês (*c*) de vez em quando (*d*) muitas vezes, (*e*) nunca, (*f*) às vezes, (*g*) todos os dias.

Documento 10: Every day.

Avaliação: (*a*) O que gosta de fazer no tempo livre? (*b*) (e.g.) Gosto de dançar. (*c*) Claro que pode. (*d*) O meu marido / a minha mulher gosta de . . . (*e*) Vejo a televisão (todos os dias . . .) (*f*) Ouvem muitas vezes a Música? (*g*) Vou à cidade para fazer compras.

Unit 9

Leitura: 1 Na ilha do Paraíso. 2 Andar. 3 No mar, três piscinas. 4 Ténis, piscinas, campo de golfe e desportos aquáticos. 5 A oportunidade de relaxar num ambiente natural e especial.

1 (*a*) Vou muitas vezes para a Itália na primavera. (*b*) Gosto da cultura italiana. (*c*) O nosso filho sempre vem connosco, mas a nossa filha prefere viajar com o namorado. (*d*) Em geral ficamos em casa, mas eu e a minha família queremos conhecer a França no outono. 2 (*a*) sei, (*b*) conhece, (*c*) sabem, (*d*) conhecem, (*e*) sei, (*f*) sabemos. 3 [possible answers] (*a*) Eu vou tirar férias em Abril. (*b*) Tu vais viajar pela Escócia o ano que vem. (*c*) Você vai visitar o meu amigo amanhã. (*d*) Nós vamos trabalhar no jardim no sábado. (*e*) Os. Senhores vão nadar no mar em Julho. (*f*) Eles vão jogar golfe na sexta-feira. 4 (*a*) Gostaria de visitar a Alemanha. (*b*) O Paulo não gostaria de trabalhar na segunda-feira. (*c*) Gostariam de beber connosco? (*d*) O meu marido/a minha mulher gostaria de provar a comida brasileira. (*e*) Gostaríamos de viajar pelos Estados Unidos. 5 All months – check list on page 90–91

Documento 11: end June – September

6 (*a*) Verdadeiro, (*b*) Falso, (*c*) Falso, (*d*) Verdadeiro,
(*e*) Verdadeiro.

Avaliação: (*a*) Onde vão passar as férias este ano? (*b*) Quero
conhecer a Grécia. (*c*) A minha família sempre passa as férias em
Portugal. (*d*) Sabe nadar? (*e*) (e.g.) O ano que vem vou passar as
férias na Itália. (*f*) Quer vir também?

Unit 10
1 geral / de / volto / dias / barato / rápido / fins / fora / vou / gosto /
bicicleta / férias / barco / avião.   2 862 / 1,241 / 349 / 2,766 / 299 /
758 / 5,512 / 10, 150 / 683 / 3,371.

Documento 12: 23747 / 29624.

Leitura: 1 Bicicleta. 2 Bonita. 3 Passear no campo, chegar mais
rápido ao trabalho e melhorar a saúde. 4 15 mil escudos. 5 Barata.

3 (*a*) Vou ao trabalho no carro do meu amigo (da minha amiga).
(b) O Paulo vai ao hospital de autocarro.   (c) A Ana viaja no
comboio das 2 e meia. (d) O senhor e a senhora da Costa vão de
férias de barco. (e) Vamos ao cinema no autocarro das 7.15.
(f) Viajas de avião? 4 (a) compre, (b) comam, (c) partam
(d) viaje, (e) falem, (f) beba.

Avaliação: (*a*) Como se chama? (*b*) Muito prazer. (*c*) Sou
inglesa, sou de Morecambe. (*a sample answer only*) (*d*) O Meu
marido/a minha mulher fala português. (*e*) Onde Moram?
(*f*) Trabalho numa universidade; sou professora. (*g*) Tenho 30 anos.
(*h*) O meu pai é alto, e honesto. (*i*) Gostas de café? (*j*) Prefiro a
França. (*k*) A minha casa é um apartamento antigo. (*l*) O sofá/a
mesa/o armário está ao lado de . . . (*m*) Que horas são? (*n*)
Levanto-me às 7 horas, vou ao trabalho, volto para casa às 5.30, janto
às 7, e deito-me às 11. (*o*) Gostam de viajar? (*p*) No tempo livre
gosto de ler. (*q*) Onde passa as férias? (*r*) Eu a minha família
gostaríamos de visitar a Espanha. (*s*) Como vai ao trabalho?
(*t*) !!!!! And take your time.

Unit 11
1 (*a*) Há autocarros para Lisboa? (*b*) A paragem de autocarros é
ali à esquerda. (*c*) O ponto de Táxis é ali à direita. (*d*) A que
horas parte o comboio para Faro? (*e*) Às seis e 15 da tarde.
(*f*) A que horas chega o barco? (*g*) Há um aeroporto aqui?

(*h*) O terminal é ali, em frente. (*i*) Para o porto se faz favor. 2
(*a*) Boa tarde, queria dois bilhetes para Loulé se faz favor. (*b*) De
ida e volta por favor. (*c*) Primeira – quanto é? (*d*) Qual é a linha
para Loulé? (*e*) A que horas parte o comboio? (*f*) E a que horas
chega? (*g*) Obrigado/a.

Documento 13: (*a*) single, (*b*) 2nd.

3 (*a*) Sim, (*b*) Castelo / catedral. (*c*) peixe / mariscos / sardinhas /
doces de amêndoa e figo. (*d*) Quinta de lago, (*e*) Não. (*f*) de
pescadores. 4 (*a*) Vire à esquerda, siga em frente, e o banco fica à
esquerda na esquina. (*b*) Vire aqui à esquerda, e depois à esquerda.
Tome a terceira rua à esquerda, e siga em frente. O mercado fica à
direita. (*c*) Vá em frente e vire à direita. Tome a primeira à direita
e siga até a estação que fica em frente. (*d*) Vire à esquerda e depois
à direita. Siga em frente, pela praça Dom João até a Rua 5 de
Outubro. Depois, vire à esquerda e vá em frente. O Turismo é ali à
direita. 5 (a) Mercado, (*b*) estação (*c*) Turismo

Unit 12
1 i (b); ii (d); iii (a); iv (c); v (e).

Notices: (*a*) for children, (*b*) no smoking, (*c*) no parking, (*d*) open
from 10-12, (*e*) danger, (*f*) emergency exit, (*g*) no entry, (*h*) closed.

Documento 14: (*a*) Park between 1 and 3 p.m. (*b*) It's an
emergency exit. 2 (*a*) esterlinas, (*b*) passaporte, (*c*) morada,
(*d*) selos, (*e*) trocar, (*f*) assinar, (*g*) cartas, (*h*) caixa.

Unit 13
Wordsearch: melancia / banana / repolho / espadarte / laranja /
carapau / pera / lulas / javalí / pimentão 1 (*a*) cenouras, (*b*) porco,
(*c*) presunto, (*d*) bolachas, (*e*) sopa, (*f*) água, (*g*) pasta de dentes,
(*h*) ovos.

Documento 15: Yes.

2 (*a*) Vários lugares – feira, centro comercial, casa de moda.
(*b*) Sim. (*c*) Não. (*d*) Uma blusa. (*e*) Azul. (*f*) Preto. (*g*) De
salto alto. (*h*) Sim, gosta. 3 (*a*) Bom dia. Queria um litro de
água e um pão de forma. (*b*) Não faz mal. Levo um. Tem presunto?
(*c*) Então, pode cortar-me seis fatias se faz favor. (*d*) Quero
também uma lata de ervilhas e uma barra de sabão. (*e*) É tudo,
obrigado/a. Quanto é?

Unit 14

1 (*a*) Paulo: uma bica, uma sandes de fiambre, um pastel de nata.
(*b*) Nuno: um galão, sandes de queijo, pastel de bacalhau, pastel de
nata. (*c*) Ana: bica, sandes de fiambre, 2 pastéis de bacalhau.
(*d*) Maria: pingado, sandes de fiambre, 2 pastéis de nata. (*e*)
Miguel: bica, pastel de bacalhau, pastel de nata. 2 (*a*) frango,
(*b*) exótica, (*c*) mexicale, (*d*) quatro estações, (*e*) neptuno 3a (*a*)
open every day, (*b*) 11.30 – 24.00 (Friday/Saturday/National
Holidays open till 2 a.m.) (*c*) Yes, to students on Mondays. 3b (*a*)
O que vais escolher? (*b*) Acho que quero uma pizza de frango. (*c*)
Tens muita fome! (*d*) Não bebes nada? (*e*) Vou pedir uma 7-Up.
(*f*) Queres um refrigerante? (*g*) Quero uma dose de batatas fritas.
4 (*a*) Boa noite, tem sopa? (*b*) Quería um caldo verde (*c*) Queria
meia dose do bacalhau. Vem com salada? (*d*) Está bem. (*e*) Pode
ser o pudim flan. (*f*) Pode ser meia gerrafa de vinho branco e depois,
uma bica. 5 (A) 10, 13 (B) 1, 16 (C) 2, 15, 18 (D) 7, 9, 12, 19
(E) 4, 8, 11, 17, 20 (F) 3, 5, 6, 14

Documento 16: Wine/water

Unit 15

1 (*a*) tenho uma dor de garganta. (*b*) A minha filha cortou o dedo.
(*c*) Doem-me os ouvidos. (*d*) O meu marido tem insolação. (*e*)
Creio que o meu filho vai vomitar. (*f*) Bati o dedo do pé. (*g*) A
minha amiga magoou a perna.

2 (*Example of completed
form*)

> George Robert Smith
>
> 56
>
> 10/3/40
>
> Newcastle, Inglaterra.
>
> 26 Church Row, Leicester, U.K.
>
> 01634 - 921550.
>
> (passport) LL01652B3.
>
> NH5288316.
>
> Mrs. J. Green, 43 Market Street
>
> Oxford, U.K.

Documento 17: Throat.

Leitura: 1 7950608. 2 Non-emergency calls. 3 National Help No. (=999). 4 424124. 5 If there's a fire (bombeiros=firemen).

Unit 16

1 (*a*) conhece, (*b*) sabemos, (*c*) conhecer, (*d*) conhecem, (*e*) sabe.

Documento 18: It was the car of the year.

2 (*a*) Este é o caminho certo para Lisboa? (*b*) Vai demorar muito? (*c*) O meu carro está avariado. (*d*) Preciso dum reboque. (*e*) Quero 8 litros de gasolina sem chumbo. (*f*) Aceita cartões de crédito? (*g*) Pode encher o depósito. 3 (*a*) Fora das cidades. (*b*) uma caixa de Pronto – Socorros. (*c*) Não. (*d*) Observar um limite de velocidade de 90 q.p.h/expor um autocolante ao vidro do carro. (*e*) 90 q.p.h. 4 pnéu / gasolina / óleo / depósito / estrada / reboque / travões / avariado.

Unit 17

1 (*a*) Tem quartos vagos? (*b*) Somos três. (*c*) Queria reservar um quarto individual. (*d*) É a pensão Sol? (*e*) Qual é o preço com pequeno almoço?

Documento 19: 1 (*a*) 2 people, (*b*) free. 2 (i) (*b*); (ii) (*d*); (iii) (*a*); (iv) (*c*); (v) (*e*)

Leitura: 1 32. 2 personal. 3 regional, the best of. 4 meaning of the art and pleasure of travel. 5 areas of rare beauty. 3 (*a*) Tem quartos vagos para hoje? (*b*) Somos três. (*c*) Vamos ficar duas noites. (*d*) Queríamos um quarto de casal e um quarto individual. (*e*) Sim, se faz favor, qual é o preço? (*f*) Está bem, obrigado/a.

Unit 18

1 (*a*) Sim. (*b*) Não. (*c*) do lago. (*d*) a chuva pinga em cima das tendas. (*e*) o fundo do parque. (*f*) 8 dias. (*g*) tudo – mercearias, jornais, garrafas de gás, coberturas impermeáveis. (*h*) 7.30 da manhã.

Documento 20: (*i*) autocarro. (*ii*) tenda pequena. (*iii*) caravana. (*iv*) carro-cama. (*v*) tenda grande. (*vi*) automóvel. 2 (*a*) F, (*b*) V, (*c*) F, (*d*) V, (*e*) F, (*f*) V.

Leitura: 1F; 2V; 3V; 4F; 5V; 6F

3 (a) iii, (b) vi, (c) iv, (d) i, (e) v, (f) ii. 4 (a) Vai fazer calor.
(b) Vai fazer sol. (c) Faz frio. (d) Vai chover. (e) Há vento.
(f) Está a nevar (há neve).

Unit 19

1a (Possible answers): (a) O Paulo foi ao parque. (b) Tu viste o
filme. (c) Eu e a Maria visitámos a cidade. (d) Vocês fizeram
muitas coisas interessantes. (e) Eu trabalhei ontem. 1b (a)
Vamos ao parque hoje? (b) Quero jogar futebol. (c) O que fizeste
ontem? (d) Fui à praia. (e) Gostou do parque, John?

Leitura: Mother: Activity 2; Father: 6; Brother: 4; Sisters: 5;
Grandparents: 7.

2 (a) A semana passada eu e a minha irmã visitámos Lisboa.
(b) Fomos a um palácio e vimos muitas coisas interessantes.
(c) Não, comemos num café na praça. (d) Sim, gostámos muito.

PORTUGUESE–ENGLISH VOCABULARY

à direita *on the right*
à esquerda *on the left*
a pé *on foot*
aborrecido *boring*
aceita *accept*
advogado/a *lawyer*
aeroporto (o) *airport*
agora *now*
agradável *agreeable*
ajuda (a) *help*
albergue (o) *hostel, inn*
alguém *someone*
ambiente (o) *atmosphere*
amigos (os) *friends*
andar (o) *floor*
anos *years*
antigo/a *old*
ao fundo *at the back*
ao lado de *next to*
aos sábados *on Saturdays*
apanhar sol *to sunbathe*
apanhar *to catch*
apartamento (o) *apartment*
aquecimento (o) *heating*
aquele/aquela *that*
aqui *here*
ar (o) *air*
areia (a) *sand*
aeroporto (o) *airport*

armário (o) *wardrobe, cupboard*
arranjar *to arrange*
arroz de marisco (o) *seafood rice*
artistico/a *artistic*
árvores (as) *trees*
às vezes *sometimes*
ascensor (o) *lift*
aspirina (a) *aspirin*
assim *so, thus*
assinar *to sign*
assoalhadas (as) *rooms*
até *until, up to*
até breve *see you soon*
atracções *attractions*
atrelado (o) *trailer*
autocarro (o) *bus*
avaria (a) *break-down*
avariado *broken down*
avenida (a) *avenue*
avião (o) *aeroplane*
azeite (o) *olive oil*

bacalhau (o) *salted cod*
bancário/a *bank clerk*
banco(o) *bank*
barato *cheap*
barco (o) *boat*
barulhento/a *noisy*
barulho (o) *noise*

bastante *quite*
bem *well*
biblioteca (a) *library*
bica (a) *espresso coffee*
bicicleta (a) *bicycle*
bilhete (o) *ticket*
blusa (a) *blouse*
boleia (a) *lift*
bonito *pretty*
botas (as) *boots*
buraco (o) *hole*

cá *here*
cabedal *leather*
cabine (a) *phone booth*
cada ... *every ...*
caixa (a) *cash desk, till*
calças (as) *trousers*
caldo verde (o) *kale soup*
calmo/a *calm*
cama (a) *bed*
caminho (o) *way, road*
camioneta (a) *coach*
camisa (a) *shirt*
campo de golfe *golf course*
campo (o) *countryside*
caravana (a) *caravan*
carne (a) *meat*
caro *expensive*
carro (o) *car*
carro-cama (o) *camper-van*
carta (a) *letter*
carteira (a) *wallet, purse*
casa de banho (a) *bathroom*
cadsa de modas (a) *fashion house*
casa (a) *house*
casal *couple, double*
cavalo (o) *horse*
cedo *early*
cenouras (as) *carrots*
centro (o) *centre*
certo *correct*
céu (o) *sky*
chamada (a) *phonecall*

chamo-me *my name is*
charmoso/a *charming*
chefe *boss*
chega *arrives*
cheio de *full of*
cheques de viagem *travellers cheques*
chuva (a) *rain*
chuveiro (o) *shower*
cidade (a) *town, city*
claro *of course*
clima (o) *climate*
coisa (a) *thing*
colecção (a) *collection*
com *with*
comboio (o) *train*
come *he / she eats*
comemos *we eat*
comida (a) *food*
como é? *what is it like?*
como está? *how are you?*
completamente *completely*
comprar *to buy*
compras (as) *shopping*
comprimido (o) *pill*
comunicar *to report*
conduzir *to drive*
conhecer *to get to know*
conjunto (o) *suit*
connosco *with us*
contra *against*
cor (a) *colour*
correio (o) *post office*
cozinha (a) *cuisine / kitchen*
creio *I believe, think*
criança (a) *child*
cuidado *careful*
cultura (a) *culture*
cultural *cultural*
custa *it costs*

de nada *don't mention it*
de onde é? *where are you from?*
de onde são? *where are you from?*
  (pl.)

de vez em quando *sometimes*
debaixo de *underneath*
deixar *to leave*
delicioso/a *delicious*
dentista (o) *dentist*
depois *then, after*
desagradável *unpleasant*
desculpa *excuse me*
desempregado/a *unemployed*
desmaiar *to faint*
desportivo/a *sporty*
desportos (os) *sports*
detrás de *behind*
difícil *difficult*
Dinamarca (a) *Denmark*
dinheiro (o) *money*
diz *says*
dona de casa *housewife*
dormir *to sleep*
dose (a) *portion*
durante *during*
dúzia (a) *dozen*

e *and*
é *is*
elegante *elegant*
elevador (o) *lift*
em *in, on*
em baixo *downstairs*
em cima de *on top of*
em cima *upstairs*
em família *as a family*
em frente de *in front of*
em geral *generally*
empresa (a) *business, company*
encantador/a *charming*
encher *to fill*
enfermeiro/a *nurse*
então *well then*
entre *in between*
escola (a) *school*
escritor/a *writer*
escritório (o) *office*
Espanha (a) *Spain*

espanhois *Spanish* (pl.)
esquina (a) *corner*
está boa? *are you well?*
estação (a) *station*
estacionado *parked*
estante (a) *bookcase*
estás bom? *are you well?*
este/esta *this*
estilo (o) *style*
estou bem *I'm well*
estou óptimo/a *I'm fine*
estrada (a) *highway*
estudante *student*
eu *I*
exactamente *exactly*
experimentar *to try on*

fácil *easy*
fala? *do you speak?*
falo *I speak*
família (a) *family*
faz favor de... *please...*
feijoada (a) *bean stew*
férias (as) *holidays*
fiambre (o) *ham*
fica *is situated*
ficar *to stay*
ficha (a) *form*
filha (a) *daughter*
filho (o) *son*
flores (as) *flowers*
fogão (o) *oven*
fome (a) *hunger*
fora *outside*
França (a) *France*
frango (o) *chicken*
freguês/esa *customer*
fresco *cooled*
frigorífico (o) *fridge*
funcionar *to work*
furo (o) *puncture*

galão (o) *milky coffee*
garrafa (a) *bottle*
gasólco (o) *diesel*

gasolina (a) *petrol*
gato (o) *cat*
gente (a) *people*
geralmente *generally*
gosta/am? *do you like?*
gostam *they like*
gostamos *we like*
gostaria de *I would like to*
gosto *I like*
grande *big*
gravata (a) *tie*
Grécia (a) *Greece*

há *there is, are*
há meia hora *½ hour ago*
havia *there was, were*
histórico *historical*
hoje *today*
Holanda (a) *Holland*
honesto/a *honest*
hotel (o) *hotel*

ida e volta *return (ticket)*
ida (a) *single (ticket)*
idade (a) *age*
ideal *ideal*
igreja (a) *church*
igualmente *likewise*
ilha (a) *island*
imenso *a lot*
incluindo *including*
informações *information*
inglês/esa *English*
inteiro *whole*
interessante *interesting*
ir *to go*
irmã (a) *sister*
irmão (o) *brother*
isolado *isolated*

Japão (o) *Japan*
jaqueta (a) *jacket*
jogar *to play*
jornais (os) *newspapers*
jovem *young*

lá fora *out there*
lá, ali *there*
lago (o) *lake*
lama (a) *mud*
lamento *I'm sorry*
laranjas (as) *oranges*
lareira (a) *fireplace*
leio *I read*
leite (o) *milk*
ler *to read*
levo *I'll take*
libras (as) *pounds*
limpar *to clean*
limpo *clean*
linha (a) *platform*
lista (a) *list, menu*
litro (o) *litre*
livros (os) *books*
loja (a) *shop*
Londres *London*
longe *a long way*
lugar (o) *place*

maçada (a) *pain, drag*
maduro *ripe*
mãe (a) *mother*
maior *bigger*
mais de *more than*
mais ou menos *more or less*
mais tarde *later*
manteiga (a) *butter*
mapa (o) *map*
máquina de lavar (a) *washing machine*
máquina fotográfica (a) *camera*
mar (o) *sea*
maravilhoso *wonderful*
marido (o) *husband*
mariscos (os) *seafood*
mas *but*
médico/a *doctor*
meio quilo *half a kilo*
melhorar *to improve*
mercearias (as) *groceries*

mesa (a) *table*
mesmo ali *right there*
moderno *modern*
molhado *wet*
mora *live*
morada (a) *address*
moram *they, you live*
moro *I live*
mosquitos (os) *mosquitoes*
movimentado *busy*
muitas vezes *often*
muito *very*
muito bem *very well*
muito prazer *pleased to meet you*
mulher (a) *wife*
muscu (o) *museum*
música (a) *music*

na *in / on the*
nadar *to swim*
namorado/a *boy / girlfriend*
não *no*
não funciona *it doesn't work*
nervoso/a *nervous*
neve (a) *snow*
nome (o) *name*
nos arredores *on the outskirts*
número (o) *number*
nunca *never*

o que faz? *what do you do?*
objectos (os) *objects*
obrigado/a *thank you*
oferece *offers*
óleo (o) *oil*
ontem *yesterday*
oportunidade (a) *opportunity*
ora bem! *well now!*
organizar *to organise*
orgulhoso/a *proud*
ou...ou... *either...or...*
ouço *I listen to*
outono (o) *Autumn*
outros (os) *the others*
ouvir *to listen to*

ovos (os) *eggs*

pacote (o) *packet*
padrão (o) *style*
pai (o) *father*
país (o) *country*
pais (os) *parents*
pão (o) *bread*
par (o) *pair*
para *in order to*
para nós *for us*
para o ano *next year*
paragem (a) *bus stop*
parede (a) *wall*
parque (o) de campismo *camping park*
parque (o) *park*
parte *departs*
partido *broken*
passamos *we spend*
passaporte (o) *passport*
passar *to pass*
passear *to stroll*
pastelaría (a) *cake shop*
pedir *to ask for*
pelo menos *at least*
pensão (a) *guest house*
pequeno/a *small*
peras (as) *pears*
perigoso *dangerous*
perto *near*
pessoalmente *personally*
picado *stung*
pingar *to drip*
pintar *to paint*
piquenique (o) *picnic*
piscina (a) *swimming pool*
planta (a) *town plan*
podem *you (pl.) can*
podemos *we can*
pode-se *you can*
pois *well*
poltrona (a) *armchair*
pôr *to put*

por noite *per night*
por favor *please*
porque *because*
porta (a) *door*
portanto *therefore*
porto (o) *port*
português/esa *Portuguese*
posso? *may I?*
postal (o) *postcard*
poucas vezes *few times, seldom*
pouquinho (um) *a little bit*
praça (a) *square*
praia (a) *beach*
preciso de *I need*
preço (o) *price*
prédio (o) *building*
preencher *to fill in*
prefere *he she, you prefer(s)*
preferem *they, you prefer*
preferimos *we prefer*
prefiro *I prefer*
preguiçoso *lazy*
presunto (o) *smoked ham*
primero *first*
problema (o) *problem*
professor *teacher*
protecção (a) *protection*
provar *to try, taste*
provavelmente *probably*
próximo *nearby*

quadra de ténis *tennis court*
quadro (o) *picture*
qual? *which?*
qualidade (a) *quality*
qualquer coisa *something*
quanto é? *how much is it?*
quantos/as *how many?*
quarto (o) *¼ litre bottle*
quarto (o) *bedroom*
que *that, which*
que mais? *what else?*
que tal? *how about?*
queijo (o) *cheese*

quem? *who?*
quer *wants*
quilo (o) *kilo*
quinze dias *fortnight*
quotidiano *everyday*

rápido *fast*
reboque (o) *lift, tow*
recepção (a) *reception*
recomendo *I recommend*
refeições (as) *meals*
reformado/a *retired*
refrigerante (o) *soft drink*
região (a) *region*
relaxante *relaxing*
remédio (o) *medicine*
repolho (o) *cabbage*
reservado *reserved*
reservar *to reserve*
resto (o) do dia *the rest of the day*
reunião (a) *meeting*
revistas (as) *magazines*
rotunda (a) *roundabout*
roubo (o) *theft*
roupas (as) *clothes*
rua (a) *road*

saia (a) *skirt*
saida (a) *exit*
sal (o) *salt*
sala de estar (a) *living room*
sala de jantar (a) *dining room*
sala (a) *living room*
salto alto *high heeled*
sandálias (as) *sandals*
sandes (a) *sandwich*
sapatos (os) *shoes*
sardinhas (as) *sardines*
saudável *healthy*
saúde (a) *health*
se *if*
se calhar *probably*
selo (o) *stamp*
sem *without*
sempre *always*

senhores (os) *you*
sentar-se *to sit down*
sentir-se *to feel*
sério/a *serious*
sim *yes*
simpático/a *nice*
sinais (os) *road signs*
sintoma (o) *symptom*
sobremesa (a) *dessert*
sofá (o) *sofa*
solitário/a *lonely*
sombra (a) *shade*
somos *we are*
sossego (o) *quiet*
sou *I am*
sou de *I am from*
sozinho *alone*
Suiça (a) *Switzerland*
sujo *dirty*
sumo (o) *fruit juice*

talvez haja *perhaps there may be*
tamanho (o) *size*
também *also*
tarde (a) *afternoon*
táxi (o) *taxi*
telenovelas (as) *soap-operas*
televisão (a) *television*
têm *they have*
tem..? *do you have..?*
temos *we have*
tempo de lazer (o) *leisure time*
tempo livre (o) *free time*
tenda (a) *tent*
tenho *I have*
terceiro *third*
terminal (o) *bus terminus*
terra (a) *land, hometown*
terraço (o) *balcony*
tipicamente *typically*
típico *typical*
tirar férias *to take a holiday*

todas as noites *every night*
todos os dias *every day*
tomar *to take*
tomaste..? *have you taken..?*
tonto *dizzy*
trabalha *you work*
trabalhador/a *hard-working*
trabalho *I work*
transeunte *passer-by*
travões (os) *brakes*
tripas (as) *tripe*
triplicado *triplicate*
trocar *to change*
trovoadas (as) *thunder*
tudo *everything*

um pouco *a bit*
um pouco de *a bit of*
uma vez por... *once a...*
único *only*
universidade(a) *university*

vagas (as) *spaces*
vago *free*
vários/as *various*
vaso (o) *vase*
velho/a *old*
vende *sells*
vende-se *for sale*
vento (o) *wind*
ver *to see, watch*
verão (o) *summer*
vestido (o) *dress*
viagem (a) *journey*
vida (a) *life*
vidro (o) *window, glass*
vir *to come*
vista (a) *view*
vive *lives*
vomitar *to be sick*

xarope (o) *syrup, remedy*

Numeros

um (uma)	1		vinte e un (uma)	21
dois (duas)	2		trinta	30
três	3		quarenta	40
quatro	4		cinquenta	50
cinco	5		sessenta	60
seis	6		setenta	70
sete	7		oitenta	80
oito	8		noventa	90
nove	9		cem (cento)	100
dez	10		cento e um (uma)	101
onze	11		duzentos/as	200
doze	12		trezentos/as	300
treze	13		quatrocentos/as	400
catorze	14		quinhentos/as	500
quinze	15		seiscentos/as	600
dezasseis	16		setecentos/as	700
dezassete	17		oitocentos/as	800
dezoito	18		novecentos/as	900
dezanove	19		mil	1 000
vinte	20		un milhâo	1 000 000

primeiro/a, 1º/1ª	*first*		sexto/a	*sixth*
segundo/a, 2º/2ª	*second*		sétimo/a	*seventh*
terceiro/a, 3º/3ª	*third*		oitavo/a	*eighth*
quarto/a, 4º/4ª	*fourth*		nono/a	*ninth*
quinto/a	*fifth*		décimo/a	*tenth*

Grammar Index